THE TURBULENT 60s

1969

**Other books in the
Turbulent 60s series:**

THE TURBULENT 60s

1969

Auriana Ojeda, *Book Editor*

Bruce Glassman, *Vice President*
Bonnie Szumski, *Publisher*
Helen Cothran, *Managing Editor*
David M. Haugen, *Series Editor*

GREENHAVEN
PRESS®

THOMSON
GALE

San Diego • Detroit • New York • San Francisco • Cleveland
New Haven, Conn. • Waterville, Maine • London • Munich

THOMSON
─────✦─────™
GALE

LIBRARY OF CONGRESS CATALOGING-IN-PUBLICATION DATA

1969 / Auriana Ojeda, book editor.
　　p. cm. — (The turbulent 60s)
　Includes bibliographical references and index.
　ISBN 0-7377-1842-0 (lib. : alk. paper) — ISBN 0-7377-1843-9 (pbk. : alk. paper)
　　1. United States—History—1961–1969—Sources. 2. Nineteen sixty-nine, A.D.—Sources. I. Ojeda, Auriana, 1977– . II. Series.
　E855.A15 2004
　973.924—dc22

2003056876

CONTENTS

FOREWORD

The 1960s were a period of immense change in America. What many view as the complacency of the 1950s gave way to increased radicalism in the 1960s. The newfound activism of America's youth turned an entire generation against the social conventions of their parents. The rebellious spirit that marked young adulthood was no longer a stigma of the outcast but rather a badge of honor among those who wanted to remake the world. And in the 1960s, there was much to rebel against in America. The nation's involvement in Vietnam was one of the catalysts that helped galvanize young people in the early 1960s. Another factor was the day-to-day Cold War paranoia that seemed to be the unwelcome legacy of the last generation. And for black Americans in particular, there was the inertia of the civil rights movement that, despite seminal victories in the 1950s, had not effectively countered the racism still plaguing the country. All of these concerns prompted the young to speak out, to decry the state of the nation that would be their inheritance.

The 1960s, then, may best be remembered for its spirit of confrontation. The student movement questioned American imperialism, militant civil rights activists confronted their elders over the slow progress of change, and the flower children faced the nation's capitalistic greed and conservative ethics and opted to create a counterculture. There was a sense of immediacy to all this activism, and people put their bodies on the line to bring about change. Although there were reactionaries and conservative holdouts, the general feeling was that a united spirit of resistance could stop the inevitability of history. People could shape their own destinies, and together they could make a better world. As sixties chronicler Todd Gitlin writes, "In the Sixties it seemed especially true that History with a capital H had come down to earth, either interfering with life or making it possible: and that within History, or threaded through it, people were living with a supercharged density: lives were bound up with one another, making claims on one another, drawing one another into the common project."

Perhaps not everyone experienced what Gitlin describes, but few would argue that the nation as a whole was left untouched by the radical notions of the times. The women's movement, the civil rights movement, and the antiwar movement left indelible marks. Even the hippie movement left behind a relaxed morality and a more ecological mindset. Popular culture, in turn, reflected these changes: Music became more diverse and experimental, movies adopted more adult themes, and fashion attempted to replicate the spirit of uninhibited youth. It seemed that every facet of American culture was affected by the pervasiveness of revolution in the 1960s, and despite the diversity of rebellions, there remained a sense that all were related to, as Gitlin puts it, "the common project."

Of course, this communal zeitgeist of the 1960s is best attributed to the decade in retrospect. The 1960s were not a singular phenomenon but a progress of individual days, of individual years. Greenhaven Press follows this rubric in The Turbulent Sixties series. Each volume of this series is devoted to the major events that define a specific year of the decade. The events are discussed in carefully chosen articles. Some of these articles are written by historians who have the benefit of hindsight, but most are contemporary accounts that reveal the complexity, confusion, excitement, and turbulence of the times. Each article is prefaced by an introduction that places the event in its historical context. Every anthology is also introduced by an essay that gives shape to the entire year. In addition, the volumes in the series contain time lines, each of which gives an at-a-glance structure to the major events of the topic year. A bibliography of helpful sources is also provided in each anthology to offer avenues for further study. With these tools, readers will better understand the developments in the political arena, the civil rights movement, the counterculture, and other facets of American society in each year. And by following the trends and events that define the individual years, readers will appreciate the revolutionary currents of this tumultuous decade—the turbulent sixties.

The Year of Breakthroughs

The year 1969 launched an era of political, social, and scientific breakthroughs at the close of a decade characterized by war, protest, and rebellion. From the battles for civil and women's rights, for example, rose Shirley Chisholm, the first African American woman elected to Congress. Chisholm shattered the glass ceiling in politics for future generations of women and African Americans. In addition, the Stonewall Riot inspired gays and lesbians to celebrate their sexuality and demand tolerance from society. One of the most celebrated events of 1969, the moon landing, ushered in an exciting new world of space exploration and technological progress. Although the sixties era was ending, these breakthroughs heralded expanded rights for women and African Americans, the gay rights movement, and technological possibility—all of which would prosper in the 1970s and beyond.

Fighter Shirley Chisholm

In her own words, Shirley Chisholm was "the first American citizen to be elected to Congress in spite of the double drawbacks of being female and having skin darkened by melanin."[1] Chisholm resembled a small schoolteacher, but her political opponents soon learned not to underestimate her intelligence or her drive. She campaigned fiercely for her appointment to Congress, and when elected, she worked tirelessly to help the underprivileged and support families and children. She credits her self-discipline and eloquence to her childhood education in the Caribbean.

Chisholm received her early education in the traditional, British-style schools of Barbados. In 1934, when she was ten years old, Chisholm moved to Brooklyn with her parents, who demanded the same self-discipline and academic excellence as her former teachers. As a result, Chisholm rose to the top of her class within a year and a half. Chisholm kept up her studies during high school and was eventually offered scholarships to attend Vassar and Oberlin colleges. She chose to attend Brooklyn College, where she decided to become a teacher. She joined clubs on campus that increased her awareness of black consciousness and the racial tension that would sweep the nation during the 1960s: "There I first heard people other than my father talk about white oppression, black racial consciousness, and black pride."[2] Her instructors and peers recognized Chisholm's unique gifts and encouraged her to pursue a career of social importance. Their encouragement strengthened her resolve to become a teacher. She believed that she could better society by helping children; however, she was also determined to participate in the burgeoning civil rights battles. Around this time, one of Chisholm's favorite professors suggested that she go into politics. According to her autobiography *Unbought and Unbossed*, Chisholm responded, "You forget two things. I'm black—and I'm a woman."[3] Although she shrugged off his suggestion, the seed that would change politics forever had been planted.

Chisholm's entrance into politics began in the early 1960s, when she participated in reorganizing New York's Seventeenth District. In 1964 she was elected to the New York State Assembly, where she served for four years. During those four years, she created a SEEK (Search for Education, Elevation, Knowledge) program that made it possible for disadvantaged young people to go to college. She also initiated a bill that created unemployment insurance for domestics and day care providers. These early actions demonstrated her lifelong commitment to helping the underprivileged and supporting families and children. Moreover, her experience as an assemblywoman prepared her for her career in Congress.

Chisholm's congressional campaign was made possible by correcting a previous wrong. When the Supreme Court ordered a reorganization of voting districts because of prior gerrymandering, a primarily African American Twelfth District of New York was created. A citizens committee interviewed many candidates and chose Chisholm as its representative. She faced stiff competition in the primary election, but with assistance and hard work, she won the primary by about one thousand votes. Her Republican challenger, James Farmer, was the former national chairman of the Congress of Racial Equality (CORE) and enjoyed a well-supported and well-financed campaign. About the time Farmer's nomination was announced, Chisholm became seriously ill. She was diagnosed as having a massive tumor. The tumor was benign, but it had to be surgically removed. In late July 1968, Chisholm underwent surgery, and after a short convalescence, she returned to her campaign. Many women's organizations offered Chisholm assistance, particularly after Farmer challenged Chisholm's competency because of her gender. Despite Farmer's money and his attempt to use her sex against her, support for Chisholm remained strong. In the November 1968 election, Chisholm defeated Farmer decisively. "He had the Liberal endorsement, but even so I drew 34,885 votes to his 13,777 combined,"[4] she states in *Unbought and Unbossed.* Congresswoman Chisholm headed for Washington in 1969.

Serving Her People

As a congresswoman, Chisholm worked tirelessly to protect programs that supported minority children and disadvantaged families. She was first assigned to the Agricultural Committee, but she fought to be appointed to a committee that she believed would better serve her constituency. She served on the Veterans Affairs Committee for two years and finally switched to the Education and Labor Committee in 1971, where she desired to serve. Chisholm campaigned for the poor, working for minimum-wage increases and federal subsidies for day care centers. She helped pass the Adequate Income Act of 1971, which guaranteed a minimum income for impoverished families. She helped convince Congress to override then-president Gerald Ford's veto of the bill, which also provided support for state day care centers. As stated by Congresswoman Barbara Lee, "[Chisholm] represented the voice of minorities, women, and children while in public office and worked hard to make sure that their issues were addressed and incorporated in all aspects of public policy."[5]

Chisholm later mounted an unsuccessful campaign for the presidency, but she is most celebrated as the person who broke through the political barriers for women and African Americans in 1969. She was elected at a time when there were few women elected officials, as well as few ethnic minorities in public office. Her efforts made political ambition and public support a reality for generations of women and African Americans to come. As of

2003, thirty-nine African Americans and seventy-six women serve in Congress. According to Congresswoman Connie Morella, "[Chisholm] broke down the barriers of race and gender relative to congressional representation. As a pioneer, an idealist, she reminds us of what true public service and political leadership could be and should be."[6]

The Stonewall Riot

While Shirley Chisholm broke through barriers in politics, another disenfranchised group, homosexuals, challenged prejudices that kept them in the margins of society. Hostility toward homosexuals had deep roots in American society. For example, state sodomy laws (that were eventually declared unconstitutional in 2003) criminalized homosexual acts. In addition, federal immigration laws excluded homosexual aliens. The 1873 Comstock Laws permitted postal authorities to exclude homosexual publications from the mail, and Hollywood's Production Code, adopted in 1934, prohibited the depiction of gay characters or open discussion of homosexuality on film. The American Psychiatric Association's (APA) diagnostic manual defined homosexuality as a psychopathology. During the Red Scare of the 1950s, the charge that homosexuals were "moral perverts"[7] and security risks led the government to exclude homosexuals from government jobs or military service. Moreover, police entrapment of homosexual men and harassment of patrons at gay bars were commonplace. In cities such as Philadelphia and Washington, D.C., police arrested as many as one hundred men per month for misdemeanor charges relating to homosexuality in the 1950s.

From this climate of repression and social disapproval sprang the Stonewall Riot. On June 27, 1969, a raid by the New York City police on the Stonewall Inn in Greenwich Village resulted in the first gay rebellion in the United States. Raids on homosexual establishments were usually met with minimal resistance, but on this occasion, the patrons of the bar retaliated against the police. Once the officers loaded the arrested patrons into a paddy wagon, a gathering crowd responded with taunts and catcalls toward the police. Suddenly, they began throwing bottles, coins, and stones at the officers, and they uprooted a parking meter and used it as a battering ram against them. The rioters barricaded the police in the bar and set it on fire, hurling objects into the broken windows. The police were rescued by reinforcements, but the rioting broke out again for four nights running. Out of the melee, thirteen people were arrested in the initial revolt, and four policemen were injured. "And yet," according to journalist Andrew Kopkind, "the Stonewall Riot must count as a transformative moment of liberation, not only for homosexuals, who were the street fighters, but for the entire sexual culture, which broke out of confinement that night as surely as gay people emerged from the closet."[8]

Stonewall's Legacy

The Stonewall Riot marked the end of the homosexual community's passive acceptance of unfair laws and social condemnation. Within the next few years, hundreds of homosexual organizations, including the Gay Liberation Front, emerged. All were dedicated to securing civil rights and greater social acceptance for gays and lesbians. The number of gay and lesbian organizations grew from around fifty in 1969 to almost eight hundred in 1973 and several thousand by 1990. In the three decades following the Stonewall rebellion, the gay rights movement won significant advances in social acceptance. By 1990, half of the states had decriminalized homosexual acts, and police harassment of homosexual establishments was reduced. Wisconsin and Massachusetts were the first states to include sexual orientation in their civil rights statutes, and many other states followed their lead. In 1975 the Civil Service Commission eliminated the ban on the employment of homosexuals in most federal jobs. Over half of the states repealed laws that criminalized same-sex behavior in the 1970s. In 1974 the APA removed homosexuality from the *Diagnostic and Statistical Manual of Mental Disorders*, and in 1981 the World Health Organization removed homosexuality from its list of illnesses. Denmark became the first country to recognize same-sex couples in 1989. Finally, in 2000 Vermont became the first U.S. state to offer same-sex couples most of the rights and privileges of marriage under new arrangements called "civil unions."

Every year in June homosexuals throughout the country commemorate the Stonewall Riot with gay pride parades. Aptly named, gay pride parades celebrate the transformation of homosexuals from shamed social outcasts to defiant protesters proudly defending their way of life. Although homosexuals still face social discrimination, the gains that have been achieved since Stonewall have dramatically improved the quality of life for gays and lesbians. As stated by Kopkind, "Lesbians and gays are surely today's children of Stonewall, but many more are stepchildren or close cousins. That June night . . . now belongs to everyone."[9]

The Moon Landing

July 20, 1969, is another moment that few participated in but now belongs to everyone. Tens of millions of people were enthralled by the grainy, black-and-white images beamed from the surface of the moon as Neil Armstrong and Edwin "Buzz" Aldrin first trod carefully, and then cavorted joyously, on another heavenly body. *Apollo 11* gave the world a memorable and nearly unanimous thrill, as people all over the planet celebrated the triumph of the first moon landing. Former president Richard Nixon later declared that it was "the greatest week in the history of the world since the Creation."[10]

Landing on the moon was a challenging process that began when President John F. Kennedy announced in a 1961 speech that the United States was dedicated to being the first nation to put a man on the moon. "I believe that this nation should commit itself to achieving the goal, before this decade is out, of landing a man on the Moon and returning him safely to the earth,"[11] Kennedy declared. One of the president's primary goals was to beat other nations to the moon, particularly the Soviet Union, and to establish America's preeminence as a scientific and technological leader. His declaration captured the American imagination and generated immense support. Apollo's success demanded the cooperation of several government officials, but by the time that the goal was accomplished in 1969, few people involved in the decision still held key positions in government. Kennedy was assassinated in 1963, and science adviser Jerome B. Wiesner left his office soon afterward. Lyndon B. Johnson succeeded Kennedy as president, but he left office in January 1969, a few months before the landing. Several other supporters of Apollo in various government agencies died or left office during the 1960s and never saw the program succeed.

Earlier Apollo missions paved the way for the success of *Apollo 11*. The first mission of public significance, *Apollo 8*, took place in 1968. The mission had been planned as a flight to test Apollo hardware in a relatively safe region close to Earth, but NASA managers obtained permission to circle the moon. In December 1968, *Apollo 8* successfully orbited the moon before splashing down in the Pacific Ocean. According to author Roger

D. Launius, "That flight was such an enormously significant accomplishment because it came at a time when American society was in crisis over Vietnam, race relations, urban problems, and a host of other difficulties. And if only for a few moments the nation united as one to focus on this epochal event."[12] Two more Apollo missions took place before the landing that tested procedures and systems to ensure the safety of *Apollo 11* astronauts and secure the success of a lunar landing.

The *Apollo 11* flight lifted off on July 16, 1969, and began the three-day trip to the moon. At 4:18 P.M., Eastern Standard Time, on July 20 the lunar module, carrying Neil Armstrong and Buzz Aldrin, landed on the moon's surface while Michael Collins orbited above in the command module. Armstrong was the first to set foot on the moon, telling millions of viewers that it was "one small step for man—one giant leap for mankind."[13] Aldrin was close on his heels, and the two men explored the lunar surface, planting an American flag in the dusty ground. They collected soil and rock samples and set up equipment for scientific experiments. The next day they launched the lunar module back to the spaceship orbiting above and began the return trip to Earth, landing in the Pacific Ocean on July 24, 1969.

Excitement over Apollo

The successful mission revived the excitement that surrounded Kennedy's announcement in the early 1960s. Parades, speaking engagements, public relations events, and a world tour all created goodwill within the United States and around the world. Through December 1972, five more missions successfully landed on the moon, each of them increasing the time spent on the lunar surface. The scientific equipment placed on the moon provided fodder for scientific discoveries and space travel in the future. As stated by Launius, the mission "demonstrated both the technological and economic virtuosity of the United States and established national preeminence over rival nations—the primary goal of the program when first envisioned by the Kennedy administration in 1961."[14] Most importantly, however, the mission brought the American people together to celebrate human achievement and the shattering of boundaries during a time of social and political upheaval. For a short time in 1969, the trauma of war and social unrest was alleviated as people joined in appreciating one of the most awe-inspiring accomplishments of all time.

The moon landing, Shirley Chisholm's appointment to Congress, and the Stonewall Riot exemplify the tremendous breakthroughs that occurred in 1969. Despite the fact that the year was torn by the Vietnam War, student protests, and radical politics, these achievements highlight the positive impact the year had on the future. As a result of Chisholm's ambition, women and African Americans enjoy the freedom to pursue political careers that were unheard of before 1969. Homosexuals can live and love openly, and many couples claim most of the rights and privileges of married couples, thanks to the defiance of the rioters at the Stonewall Inn. Finally, the moon landing opened a new world of scientific and technological achievement that has brought many more successes and even more promise of space exploration. The breakthroughs that took place at the end of an explosive decade carried the promise of an exciting new era of individual freedom and possibility.

Notes

1. Shirley Chisholm, *Unbought and Unbossed.* Boston: Houghton Mifflin, 1970, p. xi.

2. Chisholm, *Unbought and Unbossed*, p. 23.

3. Chisholm, *Unbought and Unbossed*, p. 26.

4. Chisholm, *Unbought and Unbossed*, p. 77.

5. Quoted in House of Representatives, *Recognizing Contributions, Achievements, and Dedicated Work of Shirley Anita Chisholm*, 107th Cong., 1st sess., June 12, 2001, p. 21.

6. Quoted in House of Representatives, *Recognizing Contributions, Achievements, and Dedicated Work of Shirley Anita Chisholm*, p. 24.

7. Quoted in Estelle B. Freedman, "The Historical Construction of Homosexuality in the U.S.," *Socialist Review*, Winter 1995, p. 42.

8. Andrew Kopkind, "After Stonewall," *Nation*, July 4, 1994, p. 4.

9. Kopkind, "After Stonewell," p. 6.

10. Quoted in Andrew Phillips, "Faded Dreams: Remembering the Moon Landing," *Maclean's*, July 25, 1994, p. 44.

11. John F. Kennedy, Special Message to the Congress on Urgent National Needs, delivered before a joint session of Congress, May 25, 1961.

12. Roger D. Launius, "The Legacy of Project Apollo," *Aerospace Technology Innovation*, July/August 1999, p. 3.

13. Quoted in Launius, "The Legacy of Project Apollo," p. 3.

14. Launius, "The Legacy of Project Apollo," p. 3.

The Battle of People's Park

By John Burks, John Grissim Jr., and Langdon Winner

In April students and neighbors of the University of California, Berkeley, transformed a dilapidated piece of land owned by the university into a public park. They dug up the asphalt parking lot, tilled the soil, planted trees and plants, put in a swing set and benches, and turned it into a park. Street people, elderly women and men, students, and children all joined in to make the land attractive and useful for the community. It became know as People's Park. As the park neared completion, the university, urged by then-governor Ronald Reagan, decided to reclaim the land.

On May 15, 1969, police arrested the street people who were sleeping there and sealed off an eight-block area around the park. A construction crew came in and began to fence off the park's perimeter. At noon, a rally of over six thousand people was held in nearby Sproul Plaza protesting the police occupation of the park that resulted in a riotous march to the park. Police responded with shotguns, killing one person and wounding over a hundred others. For the next two weeks, a state of insurrection existed in Berkeley: The National Guard arrived and smothered Berkeley in tear gas. The park remained fenced off. In the years immediately following, the fence around the park became a ready target whenever Berkeley erupted into protest. After a particularly raucous protest in 1972 after then-president Richard Nixon mined the harbor of Haiphong, Vietnam, the fence was torn down for the last

John Burks, John Grissim Jr., and Langdon Winner, "The Battle of People's Park," *Rolling Stone*, June 14, 1969. Copyright © 1969 by Rolling Stone, LLC. Reproduced by permission.

time and the city of Berkeley leased the land for a nominal sum and let
it be administered by a council of citizens and park habitués—the
People's Park Council. Since that time, the university has attempted to
reclaim the park land a half-dozen times or so, only to be met with protest and ultimately backing down. The following article was taken from
a 1969 issue of *Rolling Stone* magazine and gives a detailed account of
the events. Authors John Burks, John Grissim Jr., and Langdon Winner
were contributors to *Rolling Stone* at the time of publication.

People's Park was just starting to amount to something
when the war broke out. There were ten rock gardens,
several swings, sand boxes, parallel bars, monkey bars
for the kids. Over half was covered by new sod. There were three
apple trees. The first seeds in the People's Revolutionary Corn
Garden had sent down roots and had begun to sprout. The park
was sanctified by a cross section of young Berkeley clergy, and
architectural and environmental critic Alan Temko had called it
"the most significant innovation in recreational design since the
great public parks in the nineteenth and twentieth centuries."

Built by the People

Street people and Berkeley students had built it—or were building it—they had lots of plans. But now the State, propelled by
the will of a Governor [Ronald Reagan] who has vowed to put
an end to demonstrations on California campuses by any means
necessary, was going to take back People's Park. The University
had posted notices saying they planned to take back what was
theirs. The street people began circulating a "Proclamation by
Madmen" which promised that five million dollars in damage
would be done to the University if it reclaimed this one million
dollar, block-sized plot of land.

There was a lot of brave talk and the battle lines were drawn.
And the war began at 4:45 on the morning of May 15 [1969],
when 300 police cleared the park and took up positions. At 6:00
A.M., with a smallish crowd of onlookers in attendance, a seven-
man crew started at their work of erecting an eight foot steel
mesh fence around the University's "property." The crowd had
grown—and the taunting had gotten heavy—by noon when the
crew had finished.

Meanwhile, 2000 were holding a demonstration on Sproul

Plaza to decide what to do about the park. One of the final speakers was the Rev. Richard York, who ministers to street people and students out of his Free Church. "The spirit," intoned York, ornately clad in his multi-color vestment, "which built the People's Park is stronger than tear gas and clubs." The final speaker, student body president-elect Dan Siegel (who has since turned himself in on charges of inciting to riot), shouted: *"Let's go down and take the park!"*

And shortly the battle was joined.

Lethal Force

At this writing, over 256 people have been arrested, dozens have been admitted to hospitals and medical clinics, and one boy is dead.

The Alameda County Sheriff's deputies who arrived to bolster the Berkeley Police Department were armed with shotguns. According to Sheriff Frank Madigan, they were given either Number 8 or Number 9 birdshot to use. This is a critical matter, because this birdshot is somewhat smaller than a BB, and while it can do damage, it is not generally considered lethal, except possibly at close range.

But the three slugs which were dug out of a dead man who had—according to eyewitnesses—been shot by a sheriff's officer were .00 buckshot. These are huge pellets, one-third of an inch in diameter, and they can blow a hole in the side of a car.

One Dead Boy

In the case of the late James Rector, the man who was shot on a rooftop while he watched the action below on Telegraph Avenue, the buckshot did massive damage to his lower vital organs as it passed all the way up through his body to penetrate his heart. He had undergone surgery at Herrick Memorial Hospital to remove his spleen, a kidney and part of his pancreas. But the three marble-sized shot which tore all the way into his chest cavity killed him.

Jim Rector had been up to Berkeley a few times to help work on the People's Park. He lived in San Jose, 50 miles to the south, but had friends in Berkeley. On Thursday [May 15], the day the sheriff's men started blasting away with their shotguns (leaving one onlooker very likely blinded for life and many others wounded—the *San Francisco Chronicle* carried a photo of an officer firing his shotgun at a young man who is *running away* with his back turned), Rector, along with many others, had scrambled up to the rooftop to get out of the line of fire and the tear gas.

Someone on another rooftop, two buildings away, had thrown a brick. And all of a sudden, Rector told his mother at the hospital a few hours before his death, he saw an officer with a shotgun pointed at *him*. "Jim said," his mother recounts, "that he couldn't believe it was pointed at him. They hadn't done anything, thrown anything—there wasn't anything on the roof to throw. Then he said he heard a fusillade of bullets, turned sideways, and got caught in the back with the slugs."

A friend grabbed him to keep him from falling off the slanted roof. For awhile, according to another person on the same roof, a girl who works as cashier at the Cinema, they were pinned down by tear gas, and unable to carry sheets and blankets out to the wounded man, who was, by this time, bleeding profusely.

Police Assistance

Finally, after long minutes, police came up to the roof. They asked what Rector and his friend were doing there. His friend explained they'd just been watching, and that Rector was badly injured and in need of help. The cops departed without either giving any aid or sending for any. Recollections vary, but it look something between 25 minutes and an hour for an ambulance to arrive. And it came from San Leandro, about 25 miles away. When the medics got to Rector he was at zero blood pressure.

The 25-year-old with the Zapata mustache lived through the weekend, recovered enough to talk, then died at 10:25 Monday [May 19] evening.

At mid-afternoon on Thursday, Governor Ronald Reagan called in 2000 troops of the National Guard, and as police squad cars smoldered (having earlier been torched) and the cry of "We want the park! We want the park!" filled the air, they advanced in their flak suits to sweep the park, bayonets fixed. The early evening stung with shots and shouts, sirens, shattering glass, and, against this rising crescendo, the cries of the injured, 25 police among them.

Everything was perfectly staged for violence and turmoil and there was plenty of it. There were random clubbings by police throughout Friday as the demonstrators regrouped. A bit of light comedy on Saturday when a dozen National Guardsmen began wandering around and acting funny. A Guard medic discovered all of them had accepted oranges or brownies or both from hippie chicks and deduced that they had been slipped some acid. Sunday was the occasion for a free-form march through the city—with a neat surrealistic touch: the marchers planted plants and flowers along the line of march and the cop, who followed along behind, pulled up the plants, confiscating them. For what use?

The Memorial March

But Tuesday [May 20] was, in some ways, the most frightening of all, at least in its implications. Three thousand pro-Park demonstrators held a memorial march for James Rector. At 2:00 in the afternoon of a clear, warm, bright Berkeley day, some 700 stragglers had been surrounded in a tight ring on Sproul Plaza by Guardsmen.

From the second-floor balcony of the Student Union came a garbled bullhorn message from a campus cop. "Chemical agents are about to be dropped. I request that you leave the plaza."

With that, all the cops and deputies and Guardsmen put on their gas masks. Then came the whack and whine and whir of a hulking brown Sikorsky helicopter carrying a bellyful of National Guard tear gas. It came low over the treetops, no more than 200 feet, laying down a veil of white, powdery vapor for 500 yards before it got to Sproul Plaza. Brigadier General Bernard Narre, the field commander at the scene and who called in the helicopter attack, later said "It was a Godsend that it was done at that time."

From three sides, the lawmen and Guardsmen pitched tear gas into the crowd of demonstrators, who ran in all directions, screaming and shouting, trying to escape the biting, nauseating fumes. *But there was no way out.* Guardsmen had encircled the immediate area, and prevented demonstrators from getting out with the threat of their bayonets.

The light wind whipped the tear gas all over the campus and surrounding neighborhood. Students rushed out of classrooms and housewives out of their homes in a radius far from Sproul Plaza. A school picnic in Strawberry Canyon, some 40 or 50 kids enjoying the outdoors, turning to squawling, panicky chaos. The gas even seeped into Cowell Hospital, upsetting operations there, rendering nurses useless as patients gasped for breath and cried out. Said the manager of the hospital: "I protest that this is not what tear gas is for."

Chemical Warfare

All tear gas is dangerous. There is no antidote to tear gas and there have been no studies that really explain how it works. The April [1969] issue of *Today's Health*, a widely respected medical journal, tells how even mild exposure to tear gas has destroyed human eyes—though law enforcement officials always ridicule these reports. *Today's Health* is very explicit about 13 different people who had a total of 14 eyes removed following tear gas deterioration.

And, while the National Guard maintains it was using only standard tear gas, there have been reports (unconfirmed) that both vomit gas and blister gas may have been employed. The Medical Committee for Human Rights held a press conference at the Free Church to suggest this. They called it chemical warfare and said that besides regular tear gas and its tougher relative (CN), they had seen and heard of symptoms beyond these.

There had been reports, for one thing, of projectile vomiting, which, at its worst, can mean your stomach is ripped loose from its moorings and vomited up. It also causes severe and immediate diarrhea, with the further danger of shitting out your intestines. And there is the added danger, with projectile vomiting of suffocating.

Tough Talking

On the day of the attack from the sky, Governor Reagan chose to do some tough talking. He called the building of People's Park "a deliberate and planned attempt at confrontation," and defended the use of birdshot to repel it. He didn't say anything about buckshot, but he did say that cops had to fight back against the "well-armed mass of people who had stockpiled all kinds of weapons and missiles." There was no mention of it in his speech, but four tanks out of the National Guard arsenal stand ready to do combat at the Berkeley Marina, where the troops he called out are quartered.

But this is no assurance there won't be any sniping. Defending the deputies' use of shotguns, Berkeley city councilman John DeBonis, a reactionary of considerable repute locally, said: "If I had a gun and I was cornered, I'd use it." His is an argument some street people may find irresistible.

And so for days the helicopters have roared overhead, looking for trouble, leaning into endless turns, rotors thumping the spring air with a high whistle. By evening, Guardsmen cluster at streetcorners, reading, smoking, hefting rifles from shoulder to shoulder. It's impossible to find out the total number of enforcers—troops, cops, deputies, highway patrol. "We don't," chuckles Reagan's press aide Paul Beck, "want to give our troop strength away to the enemy."

Berkeley has always been the enemy to Reagan. He holds the opportunity to make it the first permanently occupied college town in the country and may prove loath to let it slip away from him.

Ask at Headquarters

Similarly, it's a round robin goose chase trying to find out who authorized the shooting. The police say it was up to the sheriff. Sheriff's office says they came in at the request of the cops. You ask a cop or a deputy who said they could shoot. "Ask at headquarters." At headquarters they tell you to check with the field commanders. Who in turn tell you to check with the guys at headquarters. You explain that you already have. "Well, then," says the grinning deputy, his badge out of sight, "move on, pal, you better move on."

The administration at Berkeley has been all but silent throughout the battle, perhaps cowed by Reagan. There have been a couple of statements, and a few appearances. But all that it comes to can be summed up in a few words Vice Chancellor Earl Cheit told a TV interviewer: "If I'd known we were going to get into guns, we'd never have gotten into this."

Chancellor Roger Heyns issued a statement to the effect that the time had come (on Tuesday, the day of the helicopter attack) to reason together to find alternatives to violence. But he proposed none.

One justification used by the authorities was that People's Park had been a noisy bother to nearby residents. In the words of Charles Glasshausser, a Berkeley resident who lives less than a block from the Park:

> I had seen the site grow from a vast mudhole parking lot into a place for people. Now I see it surrounded by a fence, by police using guns, by soldiers equipped for war. What possible justication can the University offer? It must hold itself responsible for the violent actions of previously nonviolent students. It must hold itself responsible for the conduct of policemen who fired into crowds of people.

Some 200 faculty members have agreed to stop teaching. But—sadly—there has been not a word from the Academic Senate. There seems to be a feeling that it's not worth protesting; it won't do any good and may just aggravate matters.

A Fascist Regime

University Regent Fred Dutton, one of the pre-Reagan liberals on the board, calls the Berkeley situation the "most fascistic" he has seen in this country, including Chicago at the time of the Democratic Party convention.[1] And Dutton, is no raving radical. Just a plain liberal. "Students," Dutton notes, "were planting flowers in the first place, and in the long run of history, I would have to say that flowers beat fences. And that young men beat old men every time."

How is it possible that a flower, a bush, a swing, a tree, a new park—no matter who *owns* it—could possibly damage anything or anybody? To build something on another man's land—can this be so vile an act that people must be gassed and shot and blinded and killed in consequence?

The deep thrum of the helicopters, their whirring roar continues over the occupied city, driving everybody to the brink of . . . distraction . . . beyond. . . . There is this temptation to shoot one down. You hear of the temptation from several people, from street people to straight businessmen who are joking, sort of.

"Why don't you just do it? Just get a .22 rifle and do it?"

"I'm not a violent man. I really don't believe in—you know."

"It's tempting, though."

"Well, it would take a thirty-ought-six to do the job anyway."

And the *Daily Californian*, the student newspaper, editorially toward the end of the week: "We will have that park. And we will have it or lose the university."

---

1. At the Democratic Party Convention in 1968 two student groups, the Students for a Democratic Society (SDS) and the Youth International Party (Yippies), gathered to protest the Vietnam War. Police responded with force and released tear gas on the crowd. Eight protesters were indicted for inciting a riot and conspiracy, and eight police officers were indicted for excessive force. Known as the Chicago Eight, the accused protesters were convicted, but the conviction was later overturned. The police officers were all acquitted.

The First African American Congresswoman

By Shirley Chisholm

In 1969 Shirley Chisholm became the first African American woman to serve in the U.S. Congress. In her early years in office, Chisholm worked on projects that ended the draft, increased consumer and product safety, and ended the automatic imprisonment of suspected subversives. She supported embargoes on arms sales to South Africa, day-care funding increases, and the Adequate Income Act of 1971, which guaranteed families a minimum income. She also helped to convince Congress to override President Gerald Ford's veto of support to states so that they could meet minimum day-care requirements. She worked for fair housing programs and against the creation of a Department of Education, fearing that it would result in lessening of programs for minority children. She stood against vouchers to defray the cost of going to private schools, fearing it would diminish the quality of public schools. In 1972, in an unsuccessful bid, she became the first African American, as well as the first woman, to seek a major party nomination for president of the United States. In 1984 she cofounded the National Political Congress of Black Women, and in 1993 then-president Bill Clinton nominated her to become ambassador to Jamaica, but due to poor health she withdrew her name from consideration. As the first African American congresswoman, Shirley Chisholm dismantled barri-

Shirley Chisholm, address to the U.S. House of Representatives, Washington, DC, May 21, 1969.

ers in the political arena for women and African Americans. The following selection is a speech she delivered to Congress on May 21, 1969, in which she advocates passage of the Equal Rights Amendment.

When a young woman graduates from college and starts looking for a job, she is likely to have a frustrating and even demeaning experience ahead of her. If she walks into an office for an interview, the first question she will be asked is, "Do you type?"

There is a calculated system of prejudice that lies unspoken behind that question. Why is it acceptable for women to be secretaries, librarians, and teachers, but totally unacceptable for them to be managers, administrators, doctors, lawyers, and Members of Congress.

The unspoken assumption is that women are different. They do not have executive ability, orderly minds, stability, leadership skills, and they are too emotional.

It has been observed before, that society for a long time, discriminated against another minority, the blacks, on the same basis—that they were different and inferior. The happy little homemaker and the contented "old darkey" on the plantation were both produced by prejudice.

As a black person, I am no stranger to race prejudice. But the truth is that in the political world I have been far oftener discriminated against because I am a woman than because I am black.

Prejudice against blacks is becoming unacceptable although it will take years to eliminate it. But it is doomed because, slowly, white America is beginning to admit that it exists. Prejudice against women is still acceptable. There is very little understanding yet of the immorality involved in double pay scales and the classification of most of the better jobs as "for men only."

More than half of the population of the United States is female. But women occupy only 2 percent of the managerial positions. They have not even reached the level of tokenism yet. No women sit on the AFL-CIO council or Supreme Court. There have been only two women who have held Cabinet rank, and at present there are none. Only two women now hold ambassadorial rank in the diplomatic corps. In Congress, we are down to one Senator and 10 Representatives.

Considering that there are about 3½ million more women in the United States than men, this situation is outrageous.

It is true that part of the problem has been that women have not been aggressive in demanding their rights. This was also true of the black population for many years. They submitted to oppression and even cooperated with it. Women have done the same thing. But now there is an awareness of this situation particularly among the younger segment of the population.

As in the field of equal rights for blacks, Spanish-Americans, the Indians, and other groups, laws will not change such deep-seated problems overnight. But they can be used to provide protection for those who are most abused, and to begin the process of evolutionary change by compelling the insensitive majority to reexamine it's unconscious attitudes.

The Equal Rights Amendment

It is for this reason that I wish to introduce today a proposal that has been before every Congress for the last 40 years and that sooner or later must become part of the basic law of the land — the equal rights amendment.

Let me note and try to refute two of the commonest arguments that are offered against this amendment. One is that women are already protected under the law and do not need legislation. Existing laws are not adequate to secure equal rights for women. Sufficient proof of this is the concentration of women in lower paying, menial, unrewarding jobs and their incredible scarcity in the upper level jobs. If women are already equal, why is it such an event whenever one happens to be elected to Congress?

It is obvious that discrimination exists. Women do not have the opportunities that men do. And women that do not conform to the system, who try to break with the accepted patterns, are stigmatized as "odd" and "unfeminine." The fact is that a woman who aspires to be chairman of the board, or a Member of the House, does so for exactly the same reasons as any man. Basically, these are that she thinks she can do the job and she wants to try.

A second argument often heard against the equal rights amendment is that is would eliminate legislation that many States and the Federal Government have enacted giving special protection to women and that it would throw the marriage and divorce laws into chaos.

As for the marriage laws, they are due for a sweeping reform, and an excellent beginning would be to wipe the existing ones off the books. Regarding special protection for working women, I cannot understand why it should be needed. Women need no protection that men do not need. What we need are laws to protect working people, to guarantee them fair pay, safe working conditions, protection against sickness and layoffs, and provision for dignified, comfortable retirement. Men and women need these things equally. That one sex needs protection more than the other is a male supremacist myth as ridiculous and unworthy of respect as the white supremacist myths that society is trying to cure itself of at this time.

The Stonewall Uprising and the Gay Liberation Movement

By Jack Nichols

On June 27 police raided a gay bar in New York City called the Stonewall Inn to enforce vice laws against homosexual behavior. Such raids, in which police often harassed homosexuals, were common in the 1950s and 1960s. In this instance, however, the patrons of the bar rebelled against the police, and members of the surrounding community, most of whom were also gay, joined the revolt. The ensuing demonstration, which became known as the Stonewall Rebellion, lasted for three days and spawned a newly unified and empowered homosexual community. In honor of Stonewall, gays and lesbians stage pride parades throughout the country every year in June.

In the following selection, Jack Nichols describes the gay rights movement at the time of the Stonewall riots. In 1969, he and other members of the gay community viewed Stonewall and the gay liberation movement as part of the larger counterculture intent on challenging the status quo. Regrettably, in his view, more conservative activists sought gays' assimilation into mainstream culture. Nichols is the senior editor of GayToday.com and author of *The Gay Agenda: Talking Back to Fundamentalism.*

T he Stonewall Inn [on Christopher Street in Greenwich Village, New York City], between 1967–1969, was often a fun place.

I recall a free-wheeling, colorful and democratic scene attracting a great variety of types, especially long-haired youths trying— as youths often do—to get away from their otherwise "proper" home environments and meeting gladdened refugees in flight from pre-69 Manhattan's generally unappealing gay bar circuit.

Only a few years before, I'd frequented the *Ce Soir,* one of Gotham's two gay "dance" bars where, in a back room, a light bulb hung ominously from a single cord, ignited whenever an unknown customer entered the front door.

The lighting of the bulb signaled that dancing couples must separate. In June, 1969 The Stonewall Inn was light years away from this furtive past, attracting the arrival of what media soon began calling "the new homosexual," emboldened by the 60's counterculture, by new standards challenging gender roles. Pot— the good weed—was, in those days, the drug of choice.

It was under the influence of this organic substance, in fact, that many contemplated the social revolution going on around them. It inspired assaults on inhibitions and encouraged the bold to denounce a frigid past, to look toward the creation of a new world consciousness.

Hippies, a gentle, loving, environmentally conscious, Zen-reading, LSD-gobbling, sexually communal, non-judgmental, non-violent critical mass, had upset the apple cart of social decorum. There was hope in their eyes, hope for a better future. . . .

Hoping for Sexual Integration

My own late-Sixties early-Seventies experience confirmed this boy's perspective. I began hoping—in contrast to ghetto separatists—for a final melting of gay/straight divisions and the creation of a sexually integrated society in which everybody would be free to love and make love without self-identifying through specialized sexual labels. I hoped that the developing demand for the equalization of the sexes would help bring such a world into being.

The counterculture revolution was seen by gay conservatives and by right wing politicos as a threat to the social order. The gay conservatives sought a world in which previously acceptable heterosexual standards were to be implemented in gay circles. They established gay Christian churches, sought to have their own children not through adoptions but through artificial inseminations, suggested imitation establishment marriages, and asked, along with heterosexual males, the right to fight and kill for a belligerent Vietnam-punishing Uncle Sam.

The conservatives we have with us always.

But the straight counterculture, and "the new homosexuals" were going, during the Vietnam war, in another direction, declaring themselves "gay" at the draft boards to muddle conscriptions and to denounce the war. . . .

Lige Clarke was, like me, a gay counterculture type. His observations on matrimoniacs and the crumbling institution of marriage, his concerns for suffering, starving children in an overpopulated world; his disdain for the prudish Richard Nixon and for the silly self-righteousness of established powers like the churches; his experience of the wasteful Pentagon (where he'd previously edited, with 11 security clearances, top secret messages in the office of the Army Joint Chief of Staff), made his views quite different, as were mine, from that of the gay assimilationists.

Stonewall: The Stuff of Legend

Our militant gay activism had preceded the Stonewall uprising by nearly a decade. In 1965 we'd launched picketing in Washington's direct action group, the Mattachine Society. But it was a foiled police raid on the Stonewall Inn in late June, 1969 [allegedly for liquor being served without a license], that first caught the media's attention. The Stonewall uprising offered just the right mix of dramatics: youths fighting back for the first time against police corruption, the stuff of a legend.

Almost immediately, it became clear there were those who would integrate gays into the mainstream culture and those who believed that culture to be unredeemable. As gay columnists writing for the then-zany SCREW, an otherwise straight tabloid, and for the gay newspaper, *The Advocate,* Lige Clarke and I wrote the first journalist's published accounts of the Stonewall rebellion and, because of our counterculture underpinnings, we not only celebrated it, but called on the youths of our time to press the Stonewall uprising beyond its narrow boundaries. On July 8, 1969, sounding the counterculture's view, we issued this "call to arms":

The homosexual revolution is only part of a larger revolution sweeping through all segments of society. We hope that "Gay Power" will not become a call for separation, but for sexual integration, and that the young activists will read, study, and make themselves acquainted with all of the facts which will help them to carry the sexual revolt triumphantly into the councils of the U.S. government, into the anti-homosexual churches, into the offices of anti-homosexual psychiatrists, into the city government, and into the state legislatures which make our manner of lovemaking a crime. It is time to push the homosexual revolution to its logical conclusion. We must crush tyranny wherever it exists and join forces with those who would assist in the utter destruction of the puritanical, repressive, anti-sexual Establishment.

A Vision of Liberation

We spoke, at the time, not so much of a homosexual revolution but of a revolt much larger in scope, one that addressed underlying problems like America's general difficulty facing as an extremely positive phenomenon, sexuality of all kinds. John Loughery, in his award-winning and exquisitely written history of the gay 20th century *The Other Side of Silence*, explained part of what we aimed to accomplish:

> *"This was part of a 'vision of liberation,' as novelist Michael Rumaker wrote, encompassing more than gay rights: 'The larger vision was the death of flesh hatred and shame.'"*

We hoped to see (fulfilled non-coercively) every person's natural sexual curiosity instead of its being a source of embarrassment and titillation. Pornography and possibly rape, we thought, could only thrive where sexual repression remained rampant.

"Make Love Not War," was much more than just a slogan of the times. As a counterculture theme it said that sexual repression and moronic macho posing must be dismissed because the frustrations resulting from these were root causes of a widespread militaristic mania.

Violence, in other words, was defined as the great obscenity. Former Secretary of Defense Robert McNamara's belated confession—that he'd always known that the war he'd championed was unwinnable—seems now to have justified this definition of violence. Dr. Martin Luther King, Jr.—in the midst of the government's military madness—had insisted that unconditional love would "have the final word in reality."

But America's conservative establishment would not be easily swayed, in spite of the many signs that pointed to needed change. Traditional institutions armed with vast financial resources, went on the offense, re-grouping against this splendid challenge to their oppressive programs. They would later work to discredit and muddle the counterculture's saving visions expressed through its gurus such as Theodore Rozak, Paul Goodman and Alan Watts. . . .

Gay Liberation After Stonewall

Following on the heels of avant garde feminism and the successes of the black civil rights movement, gay liberation began, after Stonewall, to gain some measure of wary recognition from a media that had deliberately ignored the earlier more peaceful picketing demonstrations at the White House, Independence Hall, the Pentagon, the Civil Service Commission and the State Department.

Michael Bakunin's anarchist slogan, "None of us are free till all of us are free," reverberated in the meetings of New York's Gay Liberation Front (GLF), established on the heels of the Stonewall rebellion. I was heartened by this, but soon became disheartened when I saw GLF fall prey to dogmatists who effectively split the energies of its idealistic membership.

The Gay Activist Alliance (GAA), (contrary to impressions given in revisionist, error-riddled histories like Martin Duberman's *Stonewall*) inherited those Stonewall energies, and GLF largely disappeared from the New York scene.

GAA, on the other hand, focused on the gay issue alone, and in a series of daring "zaps" [nonviolent, face-to-face confrontations with government and civil leaders considered homophobic] served notice through direct action that a new era was at hand. There were those of us interested in other causes and who saw how gay issues connected with them but to the Stonewall era's generation of activists, focus on gay issues, needed after long and impossible silences, seemed essential.

I made my peace with my more conservative friends by saying that the gay counterculture, on the one hand, and gay assimilationists on the other made, perhaps, two sides of a coin that, once spent, would pave the way for all same-sex lovers toward greener pastures.

But I've remained, through the years and even in the face of the gay and lesbian movement's major successes, sorry that the clear voice of the counterculture—questioning established institutions—has been mostly drowned out by a more vocal gay establishment seeking acceptance among the power players in the status quo. One of the singular values of gay liberation, therefore, gets lost, specifically its being a catalyst and encouraging, as it should for anybody who thinks about what the gay struggle reveals, skepticism about the shaky-idea foundation stones supporting the status quo. . . .

Hope for the Future

Today I marvel when I see what's been accomplished in a mere 30 years since the Stonewall uprising. Since that first gay march at The White House in 1965, when only ten people—three women and seven men (including myself)—took part, I've watched our capital city's gay and lesbian demonstrations grow size-wise over the decades—expanding into what we only dreamed about early on. I've seen a U.S. President speak out repeatedly on behalf of same-sex love and affection, and I've seen a giant community of gay men and lesbians rally to care for the sick and the wounded in this World War Three against AIDS.

Even if it is, in certain ways, a sexually-segregated community still, I continue to hope for a much-integrated future where, as prophesied by Walt Whitman, men will blur distinctions by walking hand in hand in America's streets because, as he well knew, same-sex love is not a gay matter alone, no, *"the germ is in everybody."*

Edward Kennedy Is Involved in a Fatal Car Accident

By Edward Kennedy

On Friday, July 18, Senator Edward Kennedy's car plunged off a bridge on Chappaquiddick Island near Martha's Vineyard, Massachusetts. His companion, twenty-nine-year-old Mary Jo Kopechne, was killed in the accident. Although Kennedy swam to safety, he did not report the accident until the next day, claiming that he was dazed by the crash. That delay, as well as the fuzziness of some of the details, prompted critics to suggest that Kennedy had been driving drunk, had panicked after the accident, or even had tried to arrange a cover-up of his involvement. None of these accusations, however, were ever proved. Instead Kennedy pled guilty to leaving the scene of an accident and had his driver's license revoked for a year. The following article is excerpted from Kennedy's statement regarding the accident from his father's home on July 25. Despite his explanation, the incident haunted Kennedy's image and may have been the primary obstacle that derailed his plans to run for U.S. president in 1972.

I have requested this opportunity to talk to the people of Massachusetts about the tragedy which happened last Friday evening. This morning I entered a plea of guilty to the charge of leaving the scene of an accident. Prior to my appear-

Edward Kennedy, address to the nation, July 25, 1969.

ance in court it would have been improper for me to comment on these matters. But tonight I am free to tell you what happened and to say what it means to me.

Sorting Fact from Fiction

On the weekend of July 18, I was on Martha's Vineyard Island participating with my nephew, Joe Kennedy—as for thirty years my family has participated—in the annual Edgartown Sailing Regatta. Only reasons of health prevented my wife from accompanying me.

On Chappaquiddick Island, off Martha's Vineyard, I attended, on Friday evening, July 18, a cook-out, I had encouraged and helped sponsor for devoted group of Kennedy campaign secretaries. When I left the party, around 11:15 P.M., I was accompanied by one of these girls, Miss Mary Jo Kopechne. Mary Jo was one of the most devoted members of the staff of Senator Robert Kennedy. She worked for him for four years and was broken up over his death. For this reason, and because she was such a gentle, kind, and idealistic person, all of us tried to help her feel that she still had a home with the Kennedy family.

There is not truth, not truth whatever, to the widely circulated suspicions of immoral conduct that have been leveled at my behavior and hers regarding that evening. There has never been a private relationship between us of any kind. I know of nothing in Mary Jo's conduct on that or any other occasion—the same is true of the other girls at that party—that would lend any substance to such ugly speculation about their character.

Nor was I driving under the influence of liquor.

The Sensation of Drowning

Little over one mile away, the car that I was driving on the unlit road went off a narrow bridge which had no guard rails and was built on a left angle to the road. The car overturned in a deep pond and immediately filled with water. I remember thinking as the cold water rushed in around my head that I was for certain drowning. Then water entered my lungs and I actually felt the sensation of drowning. But somehow I struggled to the surface alive.

I made immediate and repeated efforts to save Mary Jo by diving into strong and murky current, but succeeded only in increasing my state of utter exhaustion and alarm. My conduct and conversations during the next several hours, to the extent that I can remember them, make no sense to me at all.

Although my doctors informed me that I suffered a cerebral concussion, as well as shock, I do not seek to escape responsibility for my actions by placing the blame either in the physical, emotional trauma brought on by the accident, or on anyone else. I regard as indefensible the fact that I did not report the accident to the police immediately.

Instead of looking directly for a telephone after lying exhausted in the grass for an undetermined time, I walked back to the cottage where the party was being held and requested the help of two friends, my cousin, Joseph Gargan and Phil Markham, and directed them to return immediately to the scene with me—this was sometime after midnight—in order to undertake a new effort to dive down and locate Miss Kopechne. Their strenuous efforts, undertaken at some risk to their own lives, also proved futile.

Scrambled Thoughts

All kinds of scrambled thoughts—all of them confused, some of them irrational, many of them which I cannot recall, and some of which I would not have seriously entertained under normal circumstances—went through my mind during this period. They were reflected in the various inexplicable, inconsistent, and inconclusive things I said and did, including such questions as whether the girl might still be alive somewhere out of that immediate area, whether some awful curse did actually hang over all the Kennedys, whether there was some justifiable reason for me to doubt what has happened and to delay my report, whether somehow the awful weight of this incredible incident might, in some way, pass from my shoulders. I was overcome, I'm frank to say, by a jumble of emotions, grief, fear, doubt, exhaustion, panic, confusion and shock.

Instructing Gargan and Markham not to alarm Mary Jo's friends that night, I had them take me to the ferry crossing. The ferry having shut down for the night, I suddenly jumped into the water and impulsively swam across, nearly drowning once again in the effort, and returned to my hotel about 2 A.M. and collapsed in my room.

I remember going out at one point and saying something to the room clerk.

In the morning, with my mind somewhat more lucid, I made

an effort to call a family legal advisor, Burke Marshall, from a public telephone on the Chappaquiddick side of the ferry and belatedly reported the accident to the Martha's Vineyard police.

Today, as I mentioned, I felt morally obligated to plead guilty to the charge of leaving the scene of an accident. No words on my part can possibly express the terrible pain and suffering I feel over this tragic incident. This last week has been an agonizing one for me and for the members of my family, and the grief we feel over the loss of a wonderful friend will remain with us the rest of our lives.

A Senator's Credibility

These events, the publicity, innuendo, and whispers which have surrounded them and my admission of guilt this morning raises the question in my mind of whether my standing among the people of my state has been so impaired that I should resign my seat in the United States Senate. If at any time the citizens of Massachusetts should lack confidence in their Senator's character or his ability, with or without justification, he could not in my opinion adequately perform his duty and should not continue in office.

The people of this State, the State which sent John Quincy Adams, and Daniel Webster, and Charles Sumner, and Henry Cabot Lodge, and John Kennedy to the United States Senate are entitled to representation in that body by men who inspire their utmost confidence. For this reason, I would understand full well why some might think it right for me to resign. For me this will be a difficult decision to make.

It has been seven years since my first election to the Senate. You and I share many memories—some of them have been glorious, some have been very sad. The opportunity to work with you and serve Massachusetts has made my life worthwhile.

And so I ask you tonight, the people of Massachusetts, to think this through with me. In facing this decision, I seek your advice and opinion. In making it, I seek your prayers—for this is a decision that I will have finally to make on my own.

The Basis of Morality

It has been written a man does what he must in spite of personal consequences, in spite of obstacles, and dangers, and pressures, and that is the basis of human morality. Whatever may be the sacrifices he faces, if he follows his conscience—the loss of his friends, his fortune, his contentment, even the esteem of his fellow man—each man must decide for himself the course he will follow. The stories of the past courage cannot supply courage itself. For this, each man must look into his own soul.

I pray that I can have the courage to make the right decision. Whatever is decided and whatever the future holds for me, I hope that I shall have been able to put this most recent tragedy behind me and make some further contribution to our state and mankind, whether it be in public or private life.

Thank you and good night.

The Moon Landing

By Michael Collins and Edwin E. Aldrin Jr.

On July 16, *Apollo 11* launched for the moon, manned by astronauts Neil Armstrong, Edwin E. "Buzz" Aldrin Jr., and Michael Collins. On July 20, *Apollo 11* became the first spacecraft to land on the moon. Armstrong was the first man to set foot on the lunar surface, followed by Aldrin, while Collins remained in orbit above the moon. Millions of Americans tuned in to watch the landing on television and hear Armstrong's immortal words, "That's one small step for man, one giant leap for mankind." *Apollo 11*'s successful mission—to perform a lunar landing and return safely to Earth—paved the way for future space exploration and technological achievement. The following article, excerpted from Edgar M. Cortright's anthology *Apollo Expeditions to the Moon*, makes use of crew members' words, taken from books, interviews, and conferences.

*T*he splashdown May 26, 1969, of Apollo 10 cleared the way for the first formal attempt at a manned lunar landing. . . . A successful countdown test ending on July 3 showed the readiness of machines, systems, and people. The next launch window (established by lighting conditions at the landing site on Mare Tranquillitatis) opened at 9:32 A.M. EDT on July 16, 1969. The crew for Apollo 11, all of whom had already flown in space during Gemini [missions], had been intensively training as a team for many months. The following mission account makes use of crew members' own words, from books written by two of them, supplemented by space-to-ground and press-conference transcripts. . . .

Michael Collins and Edwin E. Aldrin Jr., "The Eagle Has Landed," *Apollo Expeditions to the Moon*, edited by Edgar M. Cortright. Washington, DC: Scientific and Technical Information Office, NASA, 1975.

A Magnificent Ride

ARMSTRONG: The flight started promptly, and I think that was characteristic of all events of the flight. The Saturn [rocket] gave us one magnificent ride, both in Earth orbit and on a trajectory to the Moon. Our memory of that differs little from the reports you have heard from the previous Saturn V flights.

ALDRIN: For the thousands of people watching along the beaches of Florida and the millions who watched on television, our lift-off was ear shattering. For us there was a slight increase in the amount of background noise, not at all unlike the sort one notices taking off in a commercial airliner, and in less than a minute we were traveling ahead of the speed of sound.

COLLINS: This beast is best felt. Shake, rattle, and roll! We are thrown left and right against our straps in spasmodic little jerks. It is steering like crazy, like a nervous lady driving a wide car down a narrow alley, and I just hope it knows where it's going, because for the first ten seconds we are perilously close to that umbilical tower.

ALDRIN: A busy eleven minutes later we were in Earth orbit. The Earth didn't look much different from the way it had during my first flight, and yet I kept looking at it. From space it has an almost benign quality. Intellectually one could realize there were wars underway, but emotionally it was impossible to understand such things. The thought reoccurred that wars are generally fought for territory or are disputes over borders; from space the arbitrary borders established on Earth cannot be seen. After one and a half orbits a preprogrammed sequence fired the Saturn to send us out of Earth orbit and on our way to the Moon.

ARMSTRONG: Hey Houston, Apollo 11. This Saturn gave us a magnificent ride. We have no complaints with any of the three stages on that ride. It was beautiful. . . .

Fourteen hours after liftoff, at 10:30 P.M. by Houston time, the three astronauts fasten covers over the windows of the slowly rotating command module and go to sleep. Days 2 and 3 are devoted to housekeeping chores, a small midcourse velocity correction, and TV transmissions back to Earth. In one news digest from Houston, the astronauts are amused to hear that Pravda *[a Russian newsmagazine] has referred to Armstrong as "the czar of the ship.". . .*

COLLINS: Day 4 has a decidedly different feel to it. Instead of nine hours' sleep, I get seven—and fitful ones at that. Despite our concentrated effort to conserve our energy on the way to the Moon, the pressure is overtaking us (or me at least), and I feel that all of us are aware that the honeymoon is over and we are about to lay our little pink bodies on the line. Our first shock comes as we stop our spinning motion and swing ourselves around so as to bring the Moon into view. We have not been able to see the Moon for nearly a day now, and the change is electrifying. The Moon I have known all my life, that two-dimensional small yellow disk in the sky, has gone away somewhere, to be replaced by the most awesome sphere I have ever seen. To begin with it is huge, completely filling our window. Second, it is three-dimensional. The belly of it bulges out toward us in such a pronounced fashion that I almost feel I can reach out and touch it. To add to the dramatic effect, we can see the stars again. We are in the shadow of the Moon now, and the elusive stars have reappeared.

As we ease around on the left side of the Moon, I marvel again at the precision of our path. We have missed hitting the Moon by a paltry 300 nautical miles, at a distance of nearly a quarter of a million miles from Earth, and don't forget that the Moon is a moving target and that we are racing through the sky just ahead of its leading edge. When we launched the other day the Moon was nowhere near where it is now; it was some 40 degrees of arc, or nearly 200,000 miles, behind where it is now, and yet those big computers in the basement in Houston didn't even whimper but belched out super-accurate predictions.

As we pass behind the Moon, we have just over eight minutes to go before the burn. We are super-careful now, checking and rechecking each step several times. When the moment finally arrives, the big engine instantly springs into action and reassuringly plasters us back in our seats. The acceleration is only a fraction of one G but it feels good nonetheless. For six minutes we sit there peering intent as hawks at our instrument panel, scanning the important dials and gauges, making sure that the proper thing is being done to us. When the engine shuts down, we discuss the matter with our computer and I read out the results: "Minus one, plus one, plus one." The accuracy of the overall system is phenomenal: out of a total of nearly three thousand feet per second, we have velocity errors in our body axis coordinate system of only a tenth of one foot per second in each of the three directions. That is one accurate burn, and even Neil acknowledges the fact. . . .

Asleep in Lunar Orbit

ALDRIN: We began preparing the LM [lunar module]. It was scheduled to take three hours, but because I had already started the checkout, we were completed a half hour ahead of schedule. Reluctantly we returned to the Columbia [command module] as planned. Our fourth night we were to sleep in lunar orbit. Although it was not in the flight plan, before covering the windows and dousing the lights, Neil and I carefully prepared all the equipment and clothing we would need in the morning, and mentally ran through the many procedures we would follow.

COLLINS: "Apollo 11, Apollo 11, good morning from the Black Team." Could they be talking to me? It takes me twenty seconds to fumble for the microphone button and answer groggily, I guess I have only been asleep five hours or so; I had a tough time getting to sleep, and now I'm having trouble waking up. Neil, Buzz, and I all putter about fixing breakfast and getting various items ready for transfer into the LM. [Later] I stuff Neil and Buzz into the LM along with an armload of equipment. Now I have to do the tunnel bit again, closing hatches, installing drogue and probe, and disconnecting the electrical umbilical. I am on the radio constantly now, running through an elaborate series of joint checks with Eagle. I check progress with Buzz: "I have five minutes and fifteen seconds since we started. Attitude is holding very well." "Roger, Mike, just hold it a little bit longer." "No sweat, I can hold it all day. Take your sweet time. How's the czar over there? He's so quiet." Neil chimes in, "Just hanging on—and punching." Punching those computer buttons, I guess he means. "All I can say is, beware the revolution," and then, getting no answer, I formally bid them goodbye. "You cats take it easy on the lunar surface. . . ." "O.K., Mike," Buzz answers cheerily, and I throw the switch which releases them. With my nose against the window and the movie camera churning away, I watch them go. When they are safely clear of me, I inform Neil, and he begins a slow pirouette in place, allowing me a look at his outlandish machine and its four extended legs. "The Eagle has wings," Neil exults. . . .

A Yellow Caution Light

ALDRIN: At six thousand feet above the lunar surface a yellow caution light came on and we encountered one of the few potentially serious problems in the entire flight, a problem which might have caused us to abort, had it not been for a man on the ground who really knew his job.

COLLINS: At five minutes into the burn, when I am nearly directly overhead, Eagle voices its first concern. "Program Alarm," barks Neil, "It's a 1202." What the hell is that? I don't have the alarm numbers memorized for my own computer, much less for the LM's. I jerk out my own checklist and start thumbing through it, but before I can find 1202, Houston says, "Roger, we're GO on that alarm." No problem, in other words. My checklist says 1202 is an "executive overflow," meaning simply that the computer has been called upon to do too many things at once and is forced to postpone some of them. A little farther along, at just three thousand feet above the surface, the computer flashes 1201, another overflow condition, and again the ground is superquick to respond with reassurances.

ALDRIN: Back in Houston, not to mention on board the Eagle, hearts shot up into throats while we waited to learn what would happen. We had received two of the caution lights when Steve Bales the flight controller responsible for LM computer activity, told us to proceed, through Charlie Duke, the capsule communicator. We received three or four more warnings but kept on going. When Mike, Neil, and I were presented with Medals of Freedom by President Nixon, Steve also received one. He certainly deserved it, because without him we might not have landed.

ARMSTRONG: In the final phases of the descent after a number of program alarms, we looked at the landing area and found a very large crater. This is the area we decided we would not go into; we extended the range downrange. The exhaust dust was kicked up by the engine and this caused some concern in that it degraded our ability to determine not only our altitude in the final phases but also our translational velocities over the ground. It's quite important not to stub your toe during the final phases of touchdown. . . .

ARMSTRONG: Once [we] settled on the surface, the dust settled immediately and we had an excellent view of the area surrounding the LM. We saw a crater surface, pockmarked with craters up to 15, 20, 30 feet, and many smaller craters down to a diameter of 1 foot and, of course, the surface was very fine-grained. There were a surprising number of rocks of all sizes.

A number of experts had, prior to the flight, predicted that a good bit of difficulty might be encountered by people due to the variety of strange atmospheric and gravitational characteristics. This didn't prove to be the case and after landing we felt very comfortable in the lunar gravity. It was, in fact, in our view preferable both to weightlessness and to the Earth's gravity.

When we actually descended the ladder it was found to be very much like the lunar-gravity simulations we had performed here on Earth. No difficulty was encountered in descending the ladder. The last step was about 3½ feet from the surface, and we

Astronaut Edwin E. Aldrin Jr. walks on the surface of the moon in July 1969. The photograph was taken by fellow astronaut Neil Armstrong.

were somewhat concerned that we might have difficulty in reentering the LM at the end of our activity period. So we practiced that before bringing the camera down.

ALDRIN: We opened the hatch and Neil, with me as his navigator, began backing out of the tiny opening. It seemed like a small eternity before I heard Neil say, "That's one small step for man . . . one giant leap for mankind." In less than fifteen minutes I was backing awkwardly out of the hatch and onto the surface to join Neil, who, in the tradition of all tourists, had his camera ready to photograph my arrival.

I felt buoyant and full of goose pimples when I stepped down on the surface. I immediately looked down at my feet and became intrigued with the peculiar properties of the lunar dust. If one kicks sand on a beach, it scatters in numerous directions with some grains traveling farther than others. On the Moon the dust travels exactly and precisely as it goes in various directions, and every grain of it lands nearly the same distance away.

The Boy in the Candy Store

ARMSTRONG: There were a lot of things to do, and we had a hard time getting them finished. We had very little trouble, much less trouble than expected, on the surface. It was a pleasant operation. Temperatures weren't high. They were very comfortable. The little EMU, the combination of spacesuit and backpack that sustained our life on the surface, operated magnificently. The primary difficulty was just far too little time to do the variety of things we would have liked. We had the problem of the five-year-old boy in a candy store.

ALDRIN: I took off jogging to test my maneuverability. The exercise gave me an odd sensation and looked even more odd when I later saw the films of it. With bulky suits on, we seemed to be moving in slow motion. I noticed immediately that my inertia seemed much greater. Earth-bound, I would have stopped my run in just one step, but I had to use three of four steps to sort of wind down. My Earth weight, with the big backpack and heavy suit, was 360 pounds. On the Moon I weighed only 60 pounds.

At one point I remarked that the surface was "Beautiful, beautiful. Magnificent desolation." I was struck by the contrast between the starkness of the shadows and the desert-like barrenness of the rest of the surface. It ranged from dusty gray to light tan and was unchanging except for one startling sight: our LM sitting there with its black, silver, and bright yellow-orange thermal coating shining brightly in the otherwise colorless landscape. I had seen Neil in his suit thousands of times before, but on the Moon the unnatural whiteness of it seemed unusually brilliant. We could also look around and see the Earth, which, though much larger than the Moon the Earth was seeing, seemed small—a beckoning oasis shining far away in the sky.

As the sequence of lunar operations evolved, Neil had the camera most of the time, and the majority of pictures taken on the Moon that include an astronaut are of me. It wasn't until we were back on Earth and in the Lunar Receiving Laboratory looking over the pictures that we realized there were few pictures of Neil. My fault perhaps, but we had never simulated this in our training. . . .

Voyage of Peace

ALDRIN: During a pause in experiments, Neil suggested we proceed with the flag. It took both of us to set it up and it was nearly a disaster. Public Relations obviously needs practice just as everything else does. A small telescoping arm was attached to the flagpole to keep the flag extended and perpendicular. As hard as we tried, the telescope wouldn't fully extend. Thus the flags which should have been flat, had its own unique permanent wave. Then to our dismay the staff of the pole wouldn't go far enough into the lunar surface to support itself in an upright position. After much struggling we finally coaxed it to remain upright, but in a most precarious position. I dreaded the possibility of the American flag collapsing into the lunar dust in front of the television camera.

COLLINS: [On his fourth orbital pass above] "How's it going?" "The EVA is progressing beautifully. I believe they're setting up the flag now." Just let things keep going that way, and no surprises, please. Neil and Buzz sound good, with no huffing and puffing to indicate they are overexerting themselves. But one surprise at least is in store. Houston comes on the air, not the slightest bit ruffled, and announces that the President of the United States [Richard Nixon] would like to talk to Neil and Buzz. "That would be an honor," says Neil, with characteristic dignity.

The President's voice smoothly fills the air waves with the unaccustomed cadence of the speechmaker, trained to convey inspiration, or at least emotion, instead of our usual diet of numbers and reminders. "Neil and Buzz, I am talking to you by telephone from the Oval Office at the White House, and this certainly has to be the most historic telephone call ever made. . . . Because of what you have done, the heavens have become a part of man's world. As you talk to us from the Sea of Tranquility, it inspires us to redouble our efforts to bring peace and tranquility to Earth. . . ." My God, I never thought of all this bringing peace and tranquility to anyone. As far as I am concerned, this voyage is fraught with hazards for the three of us—and especially two of us—and that is about as far as I have gotten in my thinking.

Neil, however, pauses long enough to give as well as he receives. "It's a great honor and privilege for us to be here, representing not only the United States but men of peace of all nations, and with interest and a curiosity and a vision for the future."

[Later] Houston cuts off the White House and returns to business as usual, with a long string of numbers for me to copy for future use. My God, the juxtaposition of the incongruous: roll, pitch, and yaw; prayers, peace, and tranquility. What will it be like if we really carry this off and return to Earth in one piece, with our boxes full of rocks and our heads full of new perspectives for the planet? I have a little time to ponder this as I zing off out of sight of the White House and the Earth.

ALDRIN: We had a pulley system to load on the boxes of rocks. We found the process more time-consuming and dust-scattering than anticipated. After the gear and both of us were inside, our first chore was to pressure the LM cabin and begin stowing the rock boxes, film magazines, and anything else we wouldn't need until we were connected once again with the Columbia. . . .

Liftoff from the Moon

Before beginning liftoff procedures [we] settled down for our fitful rest. We didn't sleep much at all. Among other things we were elated—and also cold. Liftoff from the Moon, after a stay totaling twenty-one hours, was exactly on schedule and fairly uneventful. The ascent stage of the LM separated, sending out a shower of brilliant insulation particles which had been ripped off from the thrust of the ascent engine. There was no time to sightsee. I was concentrating on the computers, and Neil was studying the attitude indicator, but I looked up long enough to see the flag fall over. . . . Three hours and ten minutes later we were connected once again with the Columbia.

COLLINS: I can look out through my docking reticle and see that they are steady as a rock as they drive down the center line of that final approach path. I give them some numbers. "I have 0.7 mile and I got you at 31 feet per second." We really are going to carry this off. For the first time since I was assigned to this incredible flight, I feel that it is going to happen. Granted, we are a long way from home, but from here on it should be all downhill. Within a few seconds Houston joins the conversation, with a tentative little call. "Eagle and Columbia, Houston standing by." They want to know what the hell is going on, but they don't want to interrupt us if we are in a crucial spot in our final maneuvering. Good heads! However, they needn't worry, and Neil lets them know it. "Roger, we're stationkeeping."

All Smiles and Giggles

[After docking] it's time to hustle down into the tunnel and remove hatch, probe, and drogue, so Neil and Buzz can get through. Thank God, all the claptrap works beautifully in this its final workout. The probe and drogue will stay with the LM and be abandoned with it, for we will have no further need of them and don't want them cluttering up the command module. The first one through is Buzz, with a big smile on his face. I grab his head, a hand on each temple, and am about to give him a smooch on the forehead, as a parent might greet an errant child; but then, embarrassed, I think better of it and grab his hand, and then Neil's. We cavort about a little bit, all smiles and giggles over our success, and then it's back to work as usual.

Excerpts from a TV program broadcast by the Apollo 11 astronauts on the last evening of the flight, the day before splashdown in the Pacific:

COLLINS: ". . . The Saturn V rocket which put us in orbit is an incredibly complicated piece of machinery, every piece of which worked flawlessly. This computer above my head has a 38,000-word vocabulary, each word of which has been carefully chosen to be of the utmost value to us. The SPS engine, our large rocket engine on the aft end of our service module, must have performed flawlessly or we would have been stranded in lunar orbit. The parachutes up above my head must work perfectly tomorrow or we will plummet into the ocean. We have always had confidence that this equipment will work properly. All this is possible only through the blood, sweat, and tears of a number of people.

First, the American workmen who put these pieces of machinery together in the factory. Second, the painstaking work done by various test teams during the assembly and retest after assembly. And finally, the people at the Manned Spacecraft Center, both in management, in mission planning, in flight control, and last but not least, in crew training. This operation is somewhat like the periscope of a submarine. All you see is the three of us, but beneath the surface are thousands and thousands of others, and to all of those, I would like to say, 'Thank you very much.'"

ALDRIN: ". . . This has been far more than three men on a mission to the Moon; more, still, than the efforts of a government and industry team; more, even, than the efforts of one nation. We feel that this stands as a symbol of the insatiable curiosity of all mankind to explore the unknown. Today I feel we're really fully capable of accepting expanded roles in the exploration of space. In retrospect, we have all been particularly pleased with the call signs that we very laboriously chose for our spacecraft, Columbia and Eagle. We've been pleased with the emblem of our flight, the eagle carrying an olive branch, bringing the universal symbol of peace from the planet Earth to the Moon. Personally, in reflecting on the events of the past several days, a verse from Psalms comes to mind. 'When I consider the heavens, the work of Thy fingers, the Moon and the stars, which Thou hast ordained; What is man that Thou art mindful of him?'"

ARMSTRONG: "The responsibility for this flight lies first with history and with the giants of science who have preceded this effort; next with the American people, who have, through their will, indicated their desire; next with four administrations and their Congresses, for implementing that will; and then, with the agency and industry teams that built our spacecraft, the Saturn, the Columbia, the Eagle, and the little EMU, the spacesuit and backpack that was our small spacecraft out on the lunar surface. We would like to give special thanks to all those Americans who built the spacecraft; who did the construction, design, the tests, and put their hearts and all their abilities into those craft. To those people tonight, we give a special thank you, and to all the other people that are listening and watching tonight, God bless you. Good night from Apollo 11."

The Manson Family Murders

By Dial Torgerson

On August 9 actress Sharon Tate, wife of director Roman Polanski, and four guests were brutally murdered in Tate's home in Los Angeles. The victims had been stabbed, shot, and strangled, and the murderers had scrawled the words "Pig!" and "Helter Skelter" in blood on the walls. The following night, wealthy grocery store owners Rosemary and Leno LaBianca were killed in the same gruesome fashion. Eventually the police linked the murders to the followers of cult leader Charles Manson, a career criminal who had spent most of his adult life in prison. After a ten-month trial, Manson and four members of his "family"—Susan Atkins, Leslie Van Houten, Patricia Krenwinkle, and Charles "Tex" Watson—were convicted of first-degree murder. Although Manson was not physically present during the murders, as the leader of his "family," he was viewed as the driving force behind the killings. The convicted killers were all sentenced to death, but when California briefly abolished the death penalty in 1972, they were consequently sentenced to life in prison. The Manson murders are among the most notorious crimes of the twentieth century, and Charles Manson continues to be one of the most studied killers today. The following article is the *Los Angeles Times* front page headline of the Tate murders the day after the incident. The author, Dial Torgerson, was a respected journalist, who was killed in 1983 while covering a guerrilla war in Central America.

Dial Torgerson, "Sharon Tate, Four Others Murdered," *Los Angeles Times*, August 10, 1969. Copyright © 1969 by *Los Angeles Times*. Reproduced by permission.

Film star Sharon Tate, another woman and three men were found slain Saturday, their bodies scattered around a Benedict Canyon estate in what police said resembled a ritualistic mass murder.

The victims were shot, stabbed or throttled. On the front door of the home, written in blood, was one word: "Pig."

Police arrested the only one left alive on the property—a 19-year-old houseboy. He was booked on suspicion of murder.

The Victims

Killed were:

• Miss Tate, 26, a star of "Valley of the Dolls" and wife of Roman Polanski, director of "Rosemary's Baby." She was eight months pregnant. He is in England.

• Abigail Folger, 26, heiress to the Folger's Coffee family.

• Jay Sebring, 35, once Miss Tate's fiance, a Hollywood hair stylist credited wih launching the trend to hair styling for men.

• Voityck Frokowski, 37, who worked with Polanski in Polish films before they came to Hollywood.

• Steven Parent, 18, of El Monte, who left his home Friday morning after telling his family he was going to "go to Beverly Hills."

The Crime Scene

A maid, Mrs. Winifred Chapman, went to the sprawling home at the end of Cielo Drive at 8:30 A.M. to begin her day's work. What she found sent her running to a neighbor's home in a state of shock:

In a white two-door sedan in the driveway was the body of the young man, slumped back in the driver's seat, shot to death.

On the lawn in front of the ranch-style home was the body of Frokowski.

Twenty yards away, under a fir tree on the well-trimmed lawn, was the body of Miss Folger, clad in a nightgown.

In the living room, dressed in underwear—bikini panties and a brassiere—was Miss Tate. A bloodied nylon cord was around her neck. It ran over a beam in the open-beam ceiling and was tied around the neck of Sebring, whose body lay nearby.

Over Sebring's head was a black hood. "It seemed ritualistic," said one investigating officer. Said another: "It looked like a battlefield up there."

Mrs. Chapman ran to a neighbor's home. Jim Asim, 15, was getting ready to leave the house.

"There's bodies and blood all over the place!" she cried to Asim.

The youth, who is a member of Law Enforcement Troop 800 of the Boy Scouts, called West Los Angeles police.

Enter the Police

A half-dozen police cars raced up Cielo Drive, overlooking Benedict Canyon, to the cul de sac where it ends—at the wire gate of the home at 10050 Cielo Drive rented by Polanski and Miss Tate.

The police entered the property with guns drawn. A dog bayed behind a guest house facing the driveway. Officers heard a man's voice yell to the dog to be quiet.

They entered the guest house and at gunpoint arrested William Etson Garretson, who will be 20 on August 24. He was wearing only pin-striped bell-bottom trousers.

The maid, in shock, was taken to UCLA Medical Center for treatment. Later she was taken to the West Los Angeles station, as was Garretson.

After questioning him for several hours, police booked Garretson on suspicion of murder.

Police Theory

At the scene of the crime Police Lt. Robert Madlock gave newsmen the reason:

"He was taken into custody because he was on the premises where five people were murdered."

Madlock gave few other details. Among information police did release:

Exact causes of death were not immediately determined. Autopsies were pending.

Telephone lines into the home had been cut, apparently by the murderer.

No weapon was found at the scene, although officers found pieces of what were believed to be a pistol grip inside the home.

No narcotics were found in the home. There were evidences of a struggle. There was apparently nothing missing. No motive could be immediately determined.

Dr. Thomas T. Noguchi, county coroner, went to the home Saturday afternoon. An hour later he emerged and told newsmen he couldn't elaborate beyond saying the dead were victims of "multiple wounds." He said a further announcement would probably be made today.

"This is an extraordinary case, a difficult case," he said, explaining why he came to the scene. "If my presence is demanded by the people of Los Angeles County, I'll be there."

Identifies Four Bodies

William Tenant, Miss Tate's agent, came to the home at noon—still wearing tennis clothes—and identified the bodies of Miss Tate, Miss Folger, Sebring and Frokowski.

He left, sobbing, without speaking to reporters waiting at the gate. Later he phoned Polanski at his apartment in London to inform him of Miss Tate's death.

"He broke down and cried," said a friend in London. "He made arrangements to catch the first available flight to Los Angeles."

Hollywood associates said Miss Tate had recently visited Polanski in London, where he was working on plans for a projected film.

The Society Girl

Friends said that Miss Folger had been staying at the Tate-Polanski home, where Frokowski was also a guest.

"Gibby" Folger was the daughter of Peter Folger of Woodside, California, president of the Folger Coffee Co., a subsidiary of Procter & Gamble.

She was a society girl—a graduate of Catalina School for Girls at Carmel and of Radcliffe—who had in recent months joined Miss Tate's circle of Hollywood friends, sometimes called a community of "rich hippies."

Folger told a reporter his daughter had been active in social welfare causes around Los Angeles for the past six months and "more or less commuted" between Los Angeles and the San Francisco Bay area. "She has always led a clean life," he said.

Hollywood friends told of seeing her at seance-type sessions, meditating Indian philosophies with Mia Farrow and others.

Police said that the men killed at the home were dressed in "hippie type" clothes.

The home is a rambling affair with a driveway at one side and a swimming pool at the other. The bodies were scattered from the driveway almost to the pool area.

No Escape

Police wouldn't offer any theories as to how five persons could have been killed without some of them successfully fleeing. The Ambassador auto in which the young man was killed was facing toward the gate which was the exit from the driveway.

Parent was identified by his parish priest, the Rev. Robert Byrne of the Church of the Nativity, who went to the coroner's office after the boy's father, Wilfred E. Parent, 11214 Bryant Road, El Monte, told him his son was missing.

Father Byrne began crying as Dep. Coroner Don Strickland showed him Parent's body. "Oh, my God," he said, putting his head in his hand. "Steve. Steve. Steve."

The boy's father called the coroner's office about the same time and was told that his son was dead.

Police wouldn't speculate on what an El Monte teen-ager was doing at the home of the jet-setting film crowd—but a coroner's aide said there were reports young Garretson had a guest at his caretaker's quarters Friday night, and that the guest may have been Parent.

Secluded Location

The home is secluded from others in the neighborhood. Mrs. Seymour Kott, who lives at 10170 Cielo Drive, told a reporter:

"I thought I heard some shots about midnight. About three or four. They weren't too loud. More a clap! clap! sort of thing."

Miss Tate and Polanski were married at a London registry office in January 1968. They had been separated frequently because of film commitments in various parts of the world and there had been rumors in Hollywood recently that the couple were having marital trouble.

The time of the killings wasn't immediately determined. Police told a neighbor that Miss Tate had been dead too long when the bodies were discovered for anything to be done about saving the life of her unborn child.

The Suspect

Barry Tarlow, young Garretson's attorney, said the youth told him that he was completely innocent and knew absolutely nothing of the crime. He said he had been asleep when police burst in his door with shotguns and arrested him.

Police in Garretson's hometown of Lancaster, Ohio, said he

was given a two-year suspended jail sentence in 1967 for contributing to the delinquency of a minor. His mother, Mary Garretson, 42, a divorcee, said her son had left home [in October
1968] without saying goodbye but had written saying he hoped
to return home soon.

She said he told of entertaining young friends in his caretaker's
quarters—including a young "nervous" veteran back from Vietnam whom he ordered out of the place for stealing neighbors'
champagne, and an AWOL Marine later caught and sent to the
brig.

"He's a quiet, gentle boy," the mother told The Times by
phone. "I could hit him and he'd never do a thing. I could holler
at that kid and he'd just go lie on his bed and never talk back to
me. Just lie there, quiet."

"He wrote me and phoned me often, He said he was watching
this house for this man and he wanted to quit the job as soon as
he could so he could come home. He was homesick. He left home
just after he got out of school [in 1968] and he wanted to come
home.

"He said he wanted to come home, get a car, and then maybe
go back to California and go to school, to learn to be an actor."

Garretson worked for Rudy Altabelli, who rented the home to
the Polanskis. Altabelli is in Europe and had asked Garretson to
continue his $35-a-week job as a caretaker at the property until
he came home.

"He never mentioned the people who lived there," the boy's
mother told The Times by telephone. "He did send me a picture
of that Mr. Polanski walking a dog. Bill loves dogs. He never
mentioned the lady. But he did say that Mr. Cary Grant's cook
gave him a ride up the hill once in a Rolls-Royce."

The Animals

Still at the home after Garretson was taken away were the pets
he had been helping care for: a Dalmatian, two poodles, a
Weimaraner, a Yorkshire terrier and a kitten.

The Animal Regulation Department took them away as the
coroner's office was removing the bodies of the slain.

Woodstock

By the *New Yorker*

On August 15, 16, and 17 a three-day rock music festival was held at a dairy farm near Woodstock, New York. Although only ten thousand to twenty thousand people were expected, about four hundred thousand people attended. The weekend was rainy, traffic jams up to twenty miles long slowed the highways, the facilities were overcrowded, and supplies were limited. However, the crowd shared food and water, and no violence was reported. The star lineup of performers included the Grateful Dead, Jimi Hendrix, Janis Joplin, Jefferson Airplane, The Who, Joan Baez, and many more. Many who attended Woodstock maintain that the event represented the culmination of the hippie movement—hundreds of thousands of people enjoying a weekend of peace, love, sharing, and good music. The following article from the *New Yorker* recounts one concert-goer's experience, who sums up the event in one word: "community."

I went [to Woodstock] rather casually . . . partly because I wanted to hear the music, and partly because I knew, by word of mouth, that there would be a tremendous mass of people my age, and I wanted to be part of it. Of course, there was going to be a terrific assemblage of artists—the best this kind of event has to offer—but the main thing was that by listening to the grapevine you could tell the Festival was going to be above and beyond that. We heard it wasn't going to be like Newport, with high fences, high prices, cops shoving and cursing you. We heard that there wouldn't be any reserved seats, that we'd be free to wander, and that the townspeople weren't calling out the militia in advance. I went, like the others, to meet people, to sit on the grass and play guitars, and to be together. I also knew that people were coming from thousands of miles away, but I had no idea how tremendous the event would be. We're a car culture now, and people will travel vast distances to get something they want.

The Peaceful Traffic

I drove from Rhode Island with a group of friends. When we got on the New York Thruway, we began to see the first signs of how huge it would be—Volkswagens full of kids, motorcycles, hitch-hikers carrying signs. Everybody waving at everybody else as people passed. The first traffic jam—about twenty miles from White Lake, on 17B—set the tone. It was a cheerful traffic jam. People talked from car to car. People came up and asked to sit on your hood. Somebody in our car spoke to a girl in a blue Volks next to us and, not having yet caught the tone, remarked that the jam was a drag. "Oh, no," she said quickly. "Everyone here is so beautiful." She gave us some wine, and we handed over peaches in exchange.

We inched along for two hours. Cars began parking on the roadside. Boys and girls would just sit on the hillsides with a bot-tle of wine. They had lots of time, and they were cheerful and happy. The feeling wasn't "Oh, God, what a jam!" but "Wow, look how many of us there are!" There was a gathering feeling of awe that our group was this big, that the grapevine was this big. We were exhilarated. We were in a mass of *us*.

Arrival

Finally, we got to a huge parking lot. It cost five dollars and it was already full. We were the last car in. We parked and started walking. This was 10 P.M. Thursday. There would be no music until Friday afternoon. We walked along in a stream, exchang-ing comments with every passerby. There were no houses, no lo-cal folk staring at us. People became aware of the land around us. Somebody said, "It's like being part of an encamped army that has won." We felt as though it were liberated territory. We came to the top of a hill and looked down on a huge meadow— a natural amphitheatre—where the Festival would be. In the cen-ter, people were building the stage. People were lying around in sleeping bags or sitting around little fires. The grass was fresh with dew, and the stars were bright. It was wonderful. We went on and found a campground, full of people sitting around or sleeping or eating. We unpacked our gear. For fifty cents, we bought "macroburgers" that some communal people from California had cooked. They were made of soybeans, rice, and vegetables—no meat—between slices of rye bread. The California people also gave us slices of huge cucumbers they had grown themselves. It all tasted good. The girl serving the macroburgers gave us water in a plastic cup. She said, "Save the cup. Somebody else may want it." The campground was full of the most ingenious shelters. One huge canopy was made of scraps of polyethylene fastened to scraps of wood. Beneath it about forty people were lying down, snuggled against each other, singing and playing music. There was a fence across the campground, and one tough guy—the only tough guy I saw—started to tear down the fence, but people remonstrated with him.

They told him it was the farmer's fence and it wasn't necessary to take it down. He was only allowed to take down one panel to make an exit. It was like that through the whole Festival. Where the mass needed an opening, an opening was made. There was no needless destruction. It was a functional thing. There was a woods between us and the amphitheatre. Two paths through the woods had been marked with strings of Christmas lights. One was called the Gentle Path and the other the Groovy Way. Nobody knows who named them. Late that night, we went to sleep in our sleeping bags with the sound of singing and guitars and voices all around us. I slept well.

First Day of Festivities

In the morning, it was raining lightly, but it didn't last. I went looking for water. I found a tank truck, and there I met a Rhode Island girl I knew who was there brushing her teeth. She hugged me, and the crowd laughed. We breakfasted with some people from the Santa Fe Hog Farm Commune. They were serving out of a great vat of boiled wheat and raisins, scooped onto a paper plate with a dollop of honey on it. It was delicious. It held me all day.

That day, I just wandered around. I found a group of people who were blowing up a red balloon five feet across, so that their friends could find them, but lots of other people had the same balloons, so these huge red globes dotted the fields. Various groups of people had put up amusement devices for everybody to use free. One was called the Bumblebee Nest. It consisted of forked branches ingeniously fastened together with wooden pegs to support a platform of hay. It was just for the pleasure of sitting on. Somebody had an enclosure of chickens and had brought chicken feed. It was fun to feed the chickens. Somebody else had

To many of the thousands who attended the three-day rock music festival, Woodstock represented the culmination of the hippie movement.

brought rabbits and made a big pen with benches in it, so you could sit and watch the rabbits and feed them. There was a huge tepeelike construction with a flat stone hung from ropes that you could stand on to swing. All these were free things that people had taken the trouble to provide for others. Most of the day, people wandered around and talked. I read and played cards. In the late afternoon, the music began. The amphitheatre was a mass of people, but there was no pushing. The sound system was excellent. We listened all afternoon and evening. The music was great, and the audience sang and clapped the rhythm. The performers loved it. There was a terrific feeling of unity between the crowd and the stage.

The next morning, we woke to find it raining hard. Some boys who had got soaked took off their clothes and walked around naked. It didn't bother anyone. It brought home the idea that this was our land. Nobody was busting them. I was struck by how harmless it was—how the violence of sexuality was missing. The naked boys looked harmless and innocent.

The concessionaires—hot-dog stands and so on—started out with prohibitive prices, and the kids complained to the management. All day, there were announcements from the stage about where to get free food. Eventually, there was an announcement that the concessionaires had knocked their prices down to cost.

"Don't Fight It"

It rained hard the early part of the day, but the reaction of the crowd was "Don't fight it." We sat and listened, soaking wet. The rain really did something to reinforce the spirit. There were radios on the campground, and we began to hear news reports that we were in the midst of a mass disaster. At every report, the crowd around the radio laughed. It was such a splendid example of the division between us and the outside world. It dramatized the whole crazy split that the world thought we were having a disaster and we knew we were having no such thing.

About three o'clock, the sun came out. Everyone took off his clothes to dry. I stripped to my shorts. We lay in the sun and listened to fantastic music. The most popular song was against the Vietnam war. Just as it finished, an Army helicopter flew over. The whole crowd—all those hundreds of thousands of people—looked up and waved their forefingers in the peace sign, and then gave a cheer for themselves. It was an extraordinary thing. Soon after that, the farmer who owned the land was introduced, and he got a huge cheer, too.

Late that afternoon, a "free stage" began acting as a travellers' aid, where volunteers arranged free rides for people and helped to solve problems. They took up a collection for a ten-year-old boy who had lost his money. They returned a lost child to her mother. They asked for volunteers to pick up garbage, and they made announcements warning those leaving to be careful on the way out—not to take grass with them, because of busts on the highway, and so on.

There was still another day to go, but I had to leave. We got our stuff together and jammed three hitchhikers into our car and drove it out of the mud. As we went out, people called to us, "Don't leave! Don't leave!" Nobody wanted to let go of what we'd had there. What we'd had was a fleeting, wonderful moment of what you might call "community."

Ho Chi Minh Dies

By Franz Schurmann

Ho Chi Minh, the nationalist leader of Vietnam and president of North Vietnam, died of a heart attack on September 3. He was the most famous Vietnamese revolutionary and statesman of his time. He is renowned as one of the shrewdest, most callous, dedicated, and self-abnegating leaders—a man apart in the international Communist movement.

Born in rural Vietnam in 1890, Ho Chi Minh left Vietnam in 1911 and lived in London, the United States, and France, where he became a founding member of the French Communist Party. He later lived in Moscow, but he returned to Vietnam during World War II and organized a Vietnamese independence movement, the Viet Minh. He raised an army to fight the Japanese. Subsequently, in the French Indochina War (1946–1954), he defeated the French colonial regime. After Vietnam was divided in 1954, Ho became the first president of North Vietnam. In his last years he led the north's struggle to defeat the U.S.-supported government of South Vietnam. Despite the tragedy brought by the Vietnam War, Ho remained committed to his vision of an independent Vietnam. The following article is excerpted from a respectful eulogy published two months after his death, that details Ho's accomplishments throughout his life. The author, Franz Schurmann, was a professor of history and sociology at the University of California, Berkeley, in 1969.

U ncle Ho, as every Vietnamese called him, died early in the morning of September 3 in Hanoi at the age of 79. For one week he lay in state in a glass coffin; his sandals,

Franz Schurmann, "Ho Chi Minh: A Eulogy," *Ramparts*, November 1969. Copyright © 1969 by Franz Schurmann. Reproduced by permission.

made from rubber tires, were in a small glass box at the foot of the coffin. He was buried in Hanoi's Badinh Square, where Vietnamese independence was proclaimed in August of 1945.

Obituaries giving the details of Ho's life have appeared in American papers, and their tone has been respectful but dry. None I have seen repeated Marshall Nguyen Cao Ky's venomous comment that "North Viet-Nam is now a snake without a head." Americans did not hate Ho Chi Minh the way they once did Tojo[1]—a fact which made it difficult to mobilize sentiment against the yellow hordes of North Vietnamese threatening to land on California beaches. Nor did very many Americans see him as the Red Menace, which prevented our rulers in Washington from turning the war into an old-fashioned anti-communist crusade. Broadcasts from Saigon had the South Vietnamese "man-on-the-street" saying: "Ho Chi Minh was a great man— too bad he was not on our side." The *New York Times* necrologist put his finger on the dilemma when, in his opening lines, he credited Ho Chi Minh with blending nationalism and communism. As a nationalist, Ho was good; as a communist, he was bad. So it would appear that Uncle Ho was a split personality, agonizing constantly between good ends (nationalism) and bad means (communism).

Needless to say, this is not the way Uncle Ho was seen in Viet-Nam. When he wasn't called "Uncle," he was "Chairman Ho"— the word being taken more literally there than in other socialist countries. For over half a century, he presided over the men who fought and planned for their country. His manner was that of an old rural schoolteacher lecturing his pupils. On a more cosmic plane, Ho Chi Minh was the leader of the only nation which has administered a major defeat to the United States, the greatest empire of all times.

Nations and movements have leaders for three purposes: to lead them in the daily tasks of struggle, to unify men in the face of the conflicts which always arise to divide them, and to give them a vision of that for which they fight. A great leader is a commander, a conciliator, and a man of vision. Ordinary leaders may have one of these qualities but lack the others. Lyndon B. Johnson was certainly a commander, but hardly a conciliator;

1. Hideki Tojo, late prime minister of Japan, ordered the attack on Pearl Harbor on December 7, 1941.

such vision as he had went little beyond political manipulation. His successor Richard Nixon tries hard to be a conciliator, but has yet to show any capacity to command and makes no effort to hide his lack of vision. Ho Chi Minh, in the 60 years of his life as a revolutionary fighter, had all three capacities. From his earliest days in Paris, he took the lead in organizing groups of Vietnamese exiles; again and again he undertook dangerous political missions in Asia and Europe. In the midst of these revolutionary activities, he always managed at critical times to pull bitterly quarreling factions together into a new organizational unity. Ho's ability to unify moved the Vietnamese Revolution from the Indochinese Communist Party, to the Viêt Minh, to the Democratic Republic of Viet-Nam. His spirit will ultimately unify all of Viet-Nam. While Ho Chi Minh was not a theorist, he communicated to his people in simple terms a vision which is embodied in three words repeated again and again in every declaration by the Vietnamese: independence, unity, and sovereignty. The meaning of these words (which have lost much of their moral significance in America) is both the content of Ho Chi Minh's life and the spirit of the Vietnamese Revolution.

A Revolutionary Fighter

From late adolescence to his death, Ho Chi Minh lived as a revolutionary fighter. His life can be divided into two broad periods. Until 1944, his own struggle and that of his comrades met with failure after failure—disappointments from which Ho nevertheless continually reemerged to start some new revolutionary action. After 1944, the Vietnamese Revolution finally burst through, and his life became a series of hard-won victories leading to greater challenges and then to new successes. In his biography of Ho Chi Minh, Jean Lacouture has six chapters on the first period of Ho's life, the titles of which represent various aspects of his personality: the peasant, the emigrant, the militant, the unifier, the prisoner, the liberator. The experiences which formed the personality of Ho Chi Minh during the period of failure were the elements from which the period of success evolved.

Ho Chi Minh was both in what Americans call the panhandle of Viet-Nam, just north of the DMZ [demilitarized zone]. Today the countryside is a lunar landscape produced by the most ferocious and sustained aerial bombing in history. In 1890, Nghê Tinh province was one of the poorest and most densely populated in Viet-Nam. Ho's father, who was a minor official there, was fired from his post by the French and died after a long life of wandering; his mother was a peasant.

Ho Chi Minh spent most of his life among the poor. In his early days, he lived with poor Vietnamese students. He worked as a cabin boy on a ship, a cook in London, and a photographer of family pictures in Paris. Even before he became a socialist, he had close friends among the French workers and the Africans and Arabs of Paris. In the 1930's, he was a begging monk in North-eastern Thailand, the poorest part of that country. During the ten years of war from 1944 to 1954, he lived in caves and jungle camps among his peasant fighters. For Ho, being a peasant meant living like the poor—an outlook symbolized by the sandals placed at the foot of his coffin.

A Traveling Man

In 1911 Ho left Viet-Nam for travels which did not end until 1945. Aside from political repression, the French, in collaboration with the old Vietnamese mandarins, had imposed a stifling regime on the country. The stupidity and avarice of the French colonials fitted in well with comparable characteristics of the mandarins. . . . In Viet-Nam Ho might have remained *un petit annamite*, as the French paternalistically called the people they ruled. Instead, he went to Paris where he learned to think, write and act. He also learned that to be a Vietnamese nationalist, he had to fight with the proletariats of other countries, and as a result he became one of the founding members of the French Communist Party.

When the French Socialists split after World War I, Ho went with the militants. His experiences at the Versailles Peace Conference of 1919 had propelled him into militancy. Inspired, like many other colonial peoples, by Wilson's[2] rhetoric about national self-determination, Ho had put on his best clothes and gone to the great Palace of Mirrors to present moderate demands for Vietnamese self-determination, couched in Wilsonian language. He was literally thrown out of the palace. Ho, along with many of his fellow nationals, concluded that Vietnamese independence could be achieved only through more militant action. They organized strikes, uprisings and attacks on French military gar-

2. Woodrow Wilson believed that all groups have the right to determine their own governments.

risons. Although many Vietnamese at that time yearned for the
"general uprising" which would sweep the French out of Indo-
China at one blow, Ho Chi Minh decided to take the longer road
of organization. He went to Russia and became an active agent
of the Comintern,[3] which sent him to China to help the revolutionaries there.

In the 1920's, revolutionary agitation erupted in both China
and Viet-Nam. But in 1927, Chiang Kai-shek, who had been
brought to power by a nationalist revolution, turned on the Communists and killed every one he could lay his hands on. Meanwhile the ferment in Viet-Nam continued. In Ho's own province
of Nghê Tinh, the peasants revolted and organized soviets on
land wrested from the landlords. The French responded with a
ferocious attempt to smash the movement.

As repression intensified, so did the quarrels within the revolutionary movement. The endemic tendency toward factionalism
evident everywhere in Vietnamese politics splintered the movement into minute fragments, and the French Sûreté, the secret
police, moved quickly to annihilate the fragments one by one,
crushing the revolution. In desperation, the quarreling revolutionaries appealed to Ho, then in China, to help reunify the movement. Ho's abilities as a conciliator helped, but it was too late.
Viet-Nam lay prostrate for a decade and a half. Ho was arrested
in Hong Kong in the early '30s, where he was reputed to have
died in a British prison.

A Stroke of Luck

In 1944, after spending almost a year in Chiang Kai-shek's pris-
ons, Ho got the stroke of luck he had been waiting for. Chiang, in
league with the Vietnamese Kuomintang,[4] wanted to kill him.
President [Franklin D.] Roosevelt, however, was seeking a way to
prevent the French from getting back into Indo-China. Roosevelt's
agents in China (notably the OSS [Office of Strategtic Services])
saw a way to achieve this objective by allowing Ho to organize a
liberation movement to fight both the French and the Japanese.
Thus, as a result of American pressure, Ho Chi Minh was freed.

Whatever the dark machinations of the Americans, the situa-

---

3. The Comintern—Communist International—was an organization founded by members of the
Communist Party in Russia.   4. The Kuomintang was a national political party that had its roots
in China.

tion gave Ho Chi Minh his chance. Like a good commander, he seized the opportunity. On the one hand, he organized a broad coalition of the Vietnamese nationalists then in China—called the Viêt Minh, or Viet-Nam League. On the other, he organized armed guerrilla units to start fighting in the mountains of Western Tonkin. He himself went into the mountains to lead the battle. The core of these guerrilla units was the old revolutionaries of the Indo-China Communist Party who understood the need for organization, discipline, and patient struggle. By the summer of 1945, the Americans became alarmed that Ho Chi Minh was getting too independent, that he "really was a Communist." When the Japanese withdrew in August, the general uprising that the Vietnamese revolutionaries had yearned for two decades took place. The people in the cities seized the colonial administration and welcomed Ho Chi Minh and his guerrilla bands as the liberators of Viet-Nam. In August 1945, Ho Chi Minh proclaimed the Democratic Republic of Viet-Nam.

Ho Chi Minh's brilliant success, wrested from years of failure, was short-lived. French troops again landed in Viet-Nam and with them came the old colonials, determined to bring back the good old days of French Indo-China. The French government invited Ho Chi Minh to Paris to negotiate some kind of understanding, but soon after he returned from Paris, the French colonials and their Vietnamese henchmen struck in Hanoi. Ho fled back to the hills.

Years of Barbarism

The resistance went badly during the first few years. The French did not hesitate to use the same barbarism against the Vietnamese which they themselves had, only a few years earlier, suffered at the hands of the Germans. French aircraft bombed villages and French troops burned houses—in the same way the Americans are doing now on a much larger scale.

In one day of French naval bombardment, 6000 people were killed in Haiphong. Gone was the international support that Ho had received in 1945. The Americans backed the French; Russia had other things to worry about in Eastern Europe. Mao Tse-tung's[5] forces were far away in North China fighting a civil war of their own. Each year from 1946 to 1954, the French announced

5. Mao Tse-tung was the leader of the Communist movement in China.

that the Viêt Minh was on its last leg; time and time again French statistics indicated that the last Viêt Minh soldier had been killed. But this time French repression was unable to do what it had succeeded in doing in the early 1930's.

The new unity of the Viêt Minh was symbolized by the men

Although Ho Chi Minh cultivated the image of a humble, benign "Uncle Ho," he was a shrewd and seasoned revolutionary who remained committed to his vision of an independent Vietnam.

who became Ho Chi Minh's lieutenants: Pham Van Dong, skilled at coordinating and conciliating; Vo Nguyen Giap, one of the great military commanders of the twentieth century; Lê Duan, party organizer; Truong Chinh, theoretician of revolution. Unlike the experience of the 1920's and 1930's, the leaders of the Viêt Minh developed an unbreakable solidarity which diffused a spirit of unity and struggle to all the Viêt Minh fighters. Adversity now unified rather than split the ranks of the revolutionaries. What had changed?

The most striking difference between the late '20s and the late '40s was the locus of revolutionary activity. In the '20s, the revolutionaries had met in clandestine cells in Paris, Canton and various Vietnamese cities. True, currents of mass revolutionary discontent were swirling in Viet-Nam, but the revolutionaries had no binding ties to the people. Now they were literally among peasants and mountain people, depending on them for sustenance and for fighting strength. They were not merely guests in strange villages, but comrades who aroused the spirit of revolution in those villages. Ho Chi Minh brought a spark which ignited the flames of rebellion in village after village; landlords were chased out and their land taken by the peasants; colonial officials and mandarins who had fattened themselves off the people were eliminated, often by execution; French and mercenary troops who for years had plagued the countryside were defeated in battle. Ho Chi Minh realized that revolution could not begin in Hanoi; rather it had to begin in the villages and end in Hanoi. In the '20s, the Vietnamese revolutionaries had been mainly intellectuals. In the '40s, most of the leaders of the revolution were still intellectuals, but through years of fighting they had developed a close relationship to the people.

An Organized Revolution

Ho Chi Minh learned to become a peasant revolutionary, but he was also a Communist with long experience in organization. He knew that if the revolution were not organized, the flames of rebellion would subside without contributing to the final goal: the smashing of colonial power. He also knew that while nationalism gave him widespread sympathy throughout Viet-Nam, it did not give him the troops he needed to win the war. The revolution had to be organized. Ho's field commanders turned the Viêt Minh into one of the finest fighting forces in the world, surpassed only by the National Liberation Front.[6] His party cadres built a political network reaching deep into the cities. His administrators constructed a government which operated effectively throughout Viet-Nam long before his troops marched into Hanoi in 1954. . . .

Ho Chi Minh realized that nationalism was a powerful unifying force, and that communism—in the sense of a Leninist party—provided the commanding and organizing force for the revolution and the armed struggle. But the experiences of 1946–1954 brought a third element into the picture: the liberation of the poor. Viet-Nam was controlled by a thin layer of French colonials who thrived on bureaucratic profits and the exploitation of plantations, by Vietnamese mandarins who lived on feudal sinecures, and by landlords who squeezed the peasants with impunity. The great land reform launched by the Viêt Minh in the early 1950's made the vision of the liberation of the poor a reality; it also furnished the Viêt Minh with the key weapon for their victory.

In 1953, the French decided that the time had come for the final solution. The United States, freed from the burdens of the Korean War, threw massive resources behind the French to enable them to execute their "Navarre Plan." While the Vietnamese could count on increased Chinese aid by then, their main weapon was men. The French counted on destroying the Viêt Minh regulars in a series of air-supported actions, while pacifying the villages of Tonkin through terror. Theoretically, French actions should have killed so many Viêt Minh fighters that the Viêt Minh would have melted away. In fact, however, General Giap struck back with greater manpower than ever before. No man can be coerced to fight, as the French and the Americans discovered with their own Vietnamese hirelings. Exactly as had happened in China in 1946, the radical land reform rallied the peasantry to the Viêt Minh in the most meaningful way possible: they took up arms and fought to the death for the movement led by Ho Chi Minh. . . .

The Spirit of Vietnam

From 1954 on, Ho Chi Minh became a statesman, the president of a republic, his lieutenants carrying the burden for him. He was then 64 years old, and had every right to become a venerable

6. The National Liberation Front (NLF) is a title used by nationalist, usually socialist, movements in various countries since World War II. In Viet-Nam, the National Front for the Liberation of the South (the Vietcong) was formed in 1960 to overthrow the South Vietnamese government.

schoolteacher. Immediately upon his death, the American mass media eagerly speculated on the "power struggles" which they believed would surely erupt in Hanoi. But Uncle Ho became the spirit of Viet-Nam long before his death, and it was his spirit as much as the man himself which led his people, unified them and inspired them again and again with the vision of independence, unity and sovereignty.

Uncle Ho knew that all Vietnamese wanted to be free. "The little annamites" wanted no more French colonials, no more fat landlords, mandarins or generals, no more kindly Americans helping them to happiness with bombs and dollars. (No master ever understands how much his slave wants to be free.)

Ho also knew that for centuries his people had been driven apart. Under the French, thousands of Vietnamese went abroad to work in mines and plantations. During the war against the French and the Americans, millions were driven from their homes into strange overcrowded cities and refugee camps. Vietnamese politics was traditionally a chaos of cliques and sects. Poverty and war tore families apart. Ho Chi Minh taught his people that they could get independence and unity by fighting for it, and his movement gave them the means to do so. And lastly, Ho Chi Minh told the Vietnamese that they must be sovereign.

Sovereignty means that all men must have the dignity of being masters in their own houses and respected hosts to strangers. Ho Chi Minh's first newspaper was entitled *The Pariah*, which is how he saw his own people and all others oppressed by colonialism. The yearning for dignity is one of the most powerful aspirations in men; it is the yearning to be respected by others. But one cannot command or extort respect. It must be given willingly. Ho Chi Minh knew that no amount of propaganda or begging could give the Vietnamese the respect they wanted—either from the socialist countries or from the world as a whole. The Vietnamese have fought for that dignity, that respect, and they have it today more than any other people. GI's in Viet-Nam speak respectfully of "Victor Charlie," while reviling the ARVN's.[7] The most corrupt South Vietnamese politicians cannot hide their envy of the National Liberation Front. . . . In the American mass media, Ho Chi Minh has been portrayed with a sympathy rarely

---

7. "Victor Charlie" is a military term for VC, the Vietcong. ARVN stands for the Army of the Republic of Viet-Nam, made up of South Vietnamese soldiers.

shown even to leaders of the "free world." Beyond this grudging respect from those who kill the Vietnamese, is the admiration of millions throughout the world.

One of the slogans most often seen in North Viet-Nam is "*quyet thanh*," which means "determined to win." The Vietnamese are a gentle people, often sentimental, loving leisure and the other good things in life. But inside they are stubborn to a degree which has become apparent to Americans over the years. Uncle Ho shared all these qualities of his countrymen. As the leader of the Vietnamese Revolution he was determined to win. His death has made his people even more determined to win the struggle they have fought for so long.

The Trial of the Chicago Seven Begins

By Douglas O. Linder

The Chicago Seven were seven (originally eight) defendants charged with conspiracy and inciting a riot at the 1968 Democratic National Convention, in Chicago, Illinois. The convention was the scene of massive demonstrations protesting the Vietnam War. Thousands of people showed up with signs and banners expressing their dissatisfaction with the expected nomination of Hubert Humphrey, a candidate who had remained closed mouth about the war. At first the atmosphere of the protests was rather festive, but Chicago mayor Richard Daley feared this "hippie" invasion. Daley announced a nighttime curfew and used the police to clear the streets and parks. A riot ensued. Some blamed the demonstrators for breaking the curfew and gathering without permits, but many blamed Daley and the police for abusing their authority. From the chaos, eight protesters were indicted along with eight police officers, who were charged with using excessive force to subdue the crowd. Throughout the trial, the defendants (and to a certain extent, the defense attorneys) generally mocked the court and the judge. They would not stand when the judge entered the court, they dressed informally, ate jelly beans, blew kisses at the jury, and slept. In October one of the defendants, Bobby Seale, was severed from the case and tried separately for shouting insults at the judge; hence the original Chicago

Eight became the Chicago Seven. The defendants were found guilty of both charges and sentenced to five years' imprisonment and fined five thousand dollars. However, the convictions were reversed in 1972 when it was concluded that the jury may have been biased against the defendants. The eight police officers were acquitted of all charges. In the following article, Douglas O. Linder analyzes the trial in detail. Linder is a professor of law at the University of Missouri–Kansas City.

What did it all mean? Was the Chicago Seven Trial merely, as one commentator suggested, "a monumental non-event"? Was it, as others argue, an important battle for the hearts and minds of the American people? Or is it best seen as a symbol of the conflicts of values that characterized the late sixties? These are some of the questions that surround one of the most unusual courtroom spectacles in American history, the 1969–70 trial of seven radicals accused of conspiring to incite a riot at the 1968 Democratic National Convention in Chicago.

Culturally and politically, 1968 was one of the most turbulent years America has ever seen. As the Vietnam war became the longest war in U.S. history, American casualties passed the 30,000 mark. When the Viet Cong mounted their Tet offensive [a series of coordinated attacks against cities and strongholds in South Vietnam], anti-war protests grew larger and louder on college campuses. At Columbia, students seized the office of the President and held three persons hostage to protest the school's ties to the defense Department. Two Jesuit priests, Phil and Daniel Berrigan, burned hundreds of draft records at a Selective Service center in Maryland. Following the April assassination of Martin Luther King in Memphis, riots erupted in 125 cities leaving 46 dead. After Senator Eugene McCarthy challenged incumbent President Lyndon Johnson over his support of the war, Johnson withdrew from the race. Senator Robert Kennedy entered the race after Johnson's withdrawl, only to be shot and killed on the night in June that he won the California primary. "Hair," a controversial new musical about draftees and flower children, introduced frontal nudity to large audiences. Feminists picketed the Miss America pageant, black students demanded Black Studies programs, and [Black Panther member] Eldridge Cleaver published *Soul on Ice.*

The Protests

Also in 1968, two groups met to discuss using the upcoming Democratic National Convention in Chicago to highlight their opposition to the Viet Nam War and establishment values. Although there was some loose coordination between the two groups, they had different leadership, different agendas, and favored different forms of protest and demonstrations. The more politically focused of the two groups was the National Mobilization to End the War in Vietnam (MOBE). The group more focused on promoting an uninhibited lifestyle was the Youth International Party (YIPPIES). In addition to these two groups, organizations such as the Black Panther Party and the Southern Christian Leadership Conference also planned to have representatives in Chicago to press their complaints concerning racism in American policies and politics.

Rennie Davis, the national coordinator for MOBE at the time of the Convention, first announced his intentions to come to the Democratic National Convention at a meeting of a group called "The Resistance" in November 1967, at Judd Hall at the University of Chicago. Davis told the group that he "wanted the world to know that there are thousands of young people in this country who do not want to see a rigged convention rubber-stamp another four years of Lyndon Johnson's war." Three months later the newly formed MOBE held a planning meeting in Chicago to debate four alternative strategies for the upcoming Democratic Convention: a mass disruption strategy, a strategy of uniting behind a peace candidate such as Senator Eugene McCarthy, a "stay home" strategy, and a strategy of bringing as many anti-war people as possible to Chicago for demonstrations and teach-ins. The group of about forty, including attendees Davis and Tom Hayden, generally supported the fourth strategy. In March of 1968, MOBE sponsored another meeting, this one at Lake Villa, a YMCA Camp near Chicago, to discuss plans for August. About 200 persons, including Chicago Seven defendants David Dellinger, Rennie Davis, Tom Hayden, Abbie Hoffman, and Jerry Rubin, attended the meeting. A twenty-one page document, authored by Hayden and Davis, was distributed at the meeting. The document recommended non-violence.

Meanwhile, another group was making its own plans for Chicago. The "YIPPIES" were born, and plans for a "Festival of Life" in Chicago first discussed, in December 1967. Plans for the

Festival of Life, as they were developed by Yippie founders Abbie Hoffman and Jerry Rubin, called for a "festival of youth, music, and theater." In January, the Yippies released an initial call to come to Chicago, called "A STATEMENT FROM YIP":

> Join us in Chicago in August for an international festival of youth, music, and theater. Rise up and abandon the creeping meatball! Come all you rebels, youth spirits, rock minstrels, truth-seekers, peacock-freaks, poets, barricade-jumpers, dancers, lovers and artists!
>
> It is summer. It is the last week in August, and the NATIONAL DEATH PARTY meets to bless Lyndon Johnson. We are there! There are 50,000 of us dancing in the streets, throbbing with amplifiers and harmony. We are making love in the parks. We are reading, singing, laughing, printing newspapers, groping, and making a mock convention, and celebrating the birth of FREE AMERICA in our own time.
>
> Everything will be free. Bring blankets, tents, draft-cards, body-paint, Mr. Leary's Cow, food to share, music, eager skin, and happiness. The threats of LBJ, Mayor Daley, and J. Edgar Freako [Hoover, director of the FBI] will not stop us. We are coming! We are coming from all over the world!
>
> The life of the American spirit is being torn asunder by the forces of violence, decay, and the napalm-cancer fiend. We demand the Politics of Ecstasy! We are the delicate spores of the new fierceness that will change America. We will create our own reality, we are Free America! And we will not accept the false theater of the Death Convention.
>
> We will be in Chicago. Begin preparations now! Chicago is yours! Do it!

Wild Plans

Hoffman and Rubin continued, over the next several months leading up to the Convention, to propose ever more wild plans for the Festival of Life. Rubin announced plans to nominate a pig, Pigasus the Immortal, for President. Hoffman talked about a demonstration of public fornication, calling it a "fuck-in." A Yippie Program, distributed in August of 1968, urged Festival attendees to bring "sleeping bags, extra food, blankets, bottles of

fireflies, cold cream, lots of handkerchiefs and canteens to deal
with pig spray, love beads, electric toothbrushes, see-through
blouses, manifestos, magazines, and tenacity." The program
promised poetry readings, mass meditation, "political arousal
speeches," fly casting exhibitions, rock music, and "a dawn ass-
washing ceremony." There were also activities mentioned in the
program that were somewhat problematic for the alleged conspirators' trial defense:

> Psychedelic long-haired mutant-jissomed peace leftists will con-
> sort with known dope fiends, spilling out onto the sidewalks in
> pornape disarray each afternoon. . . . Two-hundred thirty rebel
> cocksmen under secret vows are on a 24-hour alert to get the
> pants of the daughters and wifes [sic] and kept women of the
> convention delegates.

At trial, Hoffman suggested that the proposal of outlandish
events in the Yippie program and in speeches by Yippie leaders
was simply a way of having "fun." He said that no one was expected to take the events seriously.

Chicago officials, led by Mayor Richard Daley, saw the Democratic National Convention as a grand opportunity to promote
their city to the world. They resolved not to have anti-war
demonstrators spoil their plans. Pre-Convention sparring between
the City and protest groups concerned the request of the Yippies
to allow demonstrators to sleep in city parks. City Administrator
Stahl indicated on August 5, 1968, that the request for permission to sleep in the parks would be denied and that an 11 P.M. curfew would be enforced. On August 23, officials ordered city police to post signs in parks announcing the curfew. As the
Convention opening approached, Daley put the city's 12,000 police officers on twelve-hour shifts. In addition, 7,500 Army
troops and 6,000 national guardsmen, requested by Daley to aid
in keeping order, arrived in Chicago.

In late August, mostly student-age anti-war and counter-culture
activists began arriving in Chicago. Several thousand would eventually participate in the Convention week protests (a number far
below the 100,000-person estimate that some organizers had predicted). Several days before the Convention, demonstration leaders began holding classes in Lincoln Park on karate, snake dancing, and other means of self-defense. Preparations were woefully
inadequate for the level of police violence that demonstrators

would face. On Friday, August 23, MOBE learned that a federal district judge had denied their request for an injunction that would have forced the city to allow use of the parks after 11 P.M.

The next day radical leaders held a contentious meeting to discuss whether demonstrators should abide by the city's curfew. Among those favoring compliance with the curfew was Jerry Rubin; among those urging violation of the curfew was Abbie Hoffman. The first significant confrontations between demonstrators and [police] occurred that night. Some people were tear-gassed. A more serious confrontation with police was avoided when poet Allen Ginsberg led demonstrators out of Lincoln Park "Om-ing" (chanting "Ommmmmm").

The Festival of Life

Sunday, August 25 was to be the much heralded "Festival of Life" featuring rock music and Yippie revelry. Only the band MC5 showed up, but even they were reluctant to perform. They feared that police would destroy their sound system. The young people who gathered in the park on Sunday evening handed out flowers, smoked pot, made out, and listened to poetry. About 10:30, a police officer with a bullhorn walked through the park saying, "The park is closing. If you stay in the park, you'll be arrested." Some young people, most of them local "greasers" rather than out-of-town protesters, threw objects at a police car. At 11 P.M., police charged into the people still in the park, tear-gassing them and hitting them with billy clubs. The clearing of the park continued for hours. Some kids ran around smashing car windows and vandalizing buildings.

Police cracked more heads and fired more tear-gas grenades again the next night. They attacked about 3,000 demonstrators gathered in the southeastern corner of Lincoln Park shortly after the 11 P.M. curfew. Testifying later about that night, Robert Pierson, an undercover officer working as Hoffman's bodyguard, said that the Yippie leader announced, "We're going to hold the park. We're going to fuck up the pigs and the Convention." Shortly after midnight, Tom Hayden became the first of the alleged conspirators to be arrested. An officer spotted Hayden letting the air out of the tires of a police car. A half hour later, Rennie Davis (according to a prosecution undercover witness) stood at the barricades in Lincoln Park with a megaphone shouting at people to "fight the pigs."

August 27 was another wild day in Chicago. It began with a sunrise service of chants, prayers, and meditation in Lincoln Park, led by Allen Ginsberg. Bobby Seale arrived in Chicago and addressed a crowd of about 2,000 in Lincoln Park. His speech, advocating a violent response to police, was later made the basis for charging him with a violation of the 1968 Anti-Riot Act. Abbie Hoffman, furious with MOBE for its continued advocacy of non-violence, allegedly met with the Blackstone Rangers to persuade them to come to the park with weapons that night. In the Chicago Coliseum, about 4,000 persons gathered to hear David Dellinger, folk singer Phil Ochs, novelist William Burroughs and a variety of other peace movement celebrities. Shortly after 11 P.M., the nightly routine of clubbing and tear-gassing [was] repeated in the park. Some enraged demonstrators smashed windows and streetlights.

Convention week violence peaked on Wednesday, August 28. The day began with Abbie Hoffman being arrested while having breakfast and charged with public indecency for having written the word "Fuck" on his forehead. (Hoffman said he did so to discourage the press from photographing him.) In the afternoon, Dellinger, Seale, Davis, and Hayden addressed 10,000 to 15,000 demonstrators at the bandshell in Grant Park, opposite the Convention's headquarters hotel, the Conrad Hilton. Tom Hayden allegedly [told] the audience: "Make sure that if blood is going to flow, let it flow all over the city. If we're going to be disrupted and violated, let the whole stinking city be disrupted. I'll see you in the streets!" Around 3 P.M., some people in the crowd lowered an American flag from a flagpole and attempted to raise a red flag in its place. When the police move in to retrieve the American flag, Jerry Rubin yelled "Kill the pigs! Kill the cops!" In another incident, Rennie Davis was clubbed into unconsciousness, taken to a hospital, then covered with a sheet and moved from room to room in a successful effort to foil police who planned to arrest Davis during a search of the hospital. That evening, in the Chicago Amphitheatre, Democrats nominated Hubert Humphrey as their candidate for President. Police stopped a nighttime march of about 1,500 people to the Amphitheatre. They attacked demonstrators with tear gas and clubs at numerous street intersections in the area.

The clubbing and the tear-gassing finally let up on Thursday, but protest activities continued. Senator Eugene McCarthy and comedian Dick Gregory were among those who addressed a crowd in Grant Park. Police undercover officer Irwin Bock met in the park with [protesters] John Froines and Lee Weiner. Froines allegedly said that the demonstrators needed more ammunition to use against police. Weiner reportedly then suggested Molotov cocktails, adding that a good tactic might be to pick a target in the Loop and bomb it. Weiner told Bock and others to get the bottles, sand, rags, and gasoline necessary to make the Molotov cocktails.

The Trial

Until enactment of the 1968 Civil Rights Act, rioting and incitement to riot was a strictly local law enforcement issue. Congress, however, felt compelled to respond to the ever-increasing numbers of anti-war protests around the country. The new law made it a federal crime to cross state lines with the intent to incite a riot. Even after passage of the law, Attorney General Ramsey Clark and the Justice Department were reluctant to enforce the new provisions. Clark viewed what had happened in Chicago as primarily a police riot. The Attorney General expressed more interest in prosecuting police officers for brutality than in prosecuting demonstrators for rioting.

The Justice Department's lack of interest in prosecuting protest leaders outraged Chicago Mayor Richard Daley. Daley convinced a close friend and federal judge, William Campbell, to summon a grand jury to consider possible violations of the anti-riot law. On March 20, 1969, the jury returned indictments against eight demonstrators, balanced exactly by indictments against eight police officers. The eight indicted demonstrators included Abbie Hoffman, Jerry Rubin, David Dellinger, Tom Hayden, Rennie Davis, John Froines, Lee Weiner, and Bobby Seale. By the time the grand jury returned its indictments, the Nixon Administration had begun. The new attorney general, John Mitchell, exhibited none of his predecessor's reluctance about prosecuting demonstrators. Mitchell gave the green light to prosecute.

On September 24, 1969, thirteen months after the riots that shocked America, the trial of the so-called "Chicago Eight" began in the oak-panelled, twenty-third-floor courtroom of Judge Julius Hoffman. The 300 members of the panel of potential jurors were overwhelmingly white, middle-class and middle-aged. They reminded author and trial observer J. Anthony Lukas of "the Rolling Meadows Bowling League lost on their way to the

lanes." Defense attorneys William Kunstler and Leonard Weinglass submitted to Judge Hoffman a list of fifty-four proposed
questions for potential jurors. They believed that the questions
might aid them in their use of juror challenges by revealing cultural biases. Among the questions the defense attorneys wanted
to ask jurors were: "Do you know who Janis Joplin and Jimi
Hendrix are?", "Would you let your son or daughter marry a Yippie?", and "If your children are female, do they wear brassieres
all the time?" Judge Hoffman rejected all but one of the proposed
questions, asking the jurors only "Are you, or do you have any
close friends or relatives who are employed by any law enforcement agencies?" (Later, the Seventh Circuit Court of Appeals
would cite the judge's refusal to allow inquiry, into the potential
cultural biases of jurors as a ground for reversing all convictions.)
Three hours after voir dire [preliminary examination of jurors
and witnesses] began, a jury of two white men and ten women,
two black and eight white, was seated. It was clearly not a good
jury for the defense. (After the trial, one female juror commented
that the defendants "should be convicted for their appearance,
their language and their lifestyle." Edward Kratzke, the jury foreman, also was angered by the defendants' courtroom behavior:
"These defendants wouldn't even stand up when the judge
walked in; when there is no more respect we might as well give
up the United States." A third juror expressed the view that the
demonstrators "should have been shot down by the police.")

The defense and prosecution tables stood in dramatic contrast.
At the defense table, defendants relaxed in blue jeans and sweat-
shirts, often with their feet up on chairs or the table itself. Hoffman and Rubin favored attire that included headbands, buttons,
beads, and colorful shirts. The defendants passed trial hours
munching jelly beans, cracking jokes, offering editorial comments, making faces, reading newspapers, and sleeping. The area
around the defense table was littered with clothing, candy wrap-
pers, and even (on one day) a package of marijuana. The prosecution table, behind which sat silver-haired District Attorney
Thomas Foran and his young assistant Richard Shultz in their
business suits, was, on the other hand, a picture of neatness and
efficiency. The prosecution table was clear of all but carefully
arranged notes, a file of index cards, and a pencil.

There was division in the defense ranks concerning trial strategy. Some of the defendants, such as Tom Hayden, wanted to

play the trial straight: to concentrate on winning jurors by diligently pursuing weaknesses in the prosecution's case and by observing a degree of courtroom decorum. Others, such as Jerry Rubin and Abbie Hoffman, saw the trial as an opportunity to appeal to young people around the country. They wanted to turn the trial into entertaining theater that would receive maximum attention in the press. To that end, the Yippies would spice up the days of the trial by, for example, wearing judicial robes, bringing into the courtroom a birthday cake, blowing kisses to the jury, baring their chests, or placing the flag of the National Liberation Front on the defense table.

In his trial account *The Barnyard Epithet and Other Obscenities*, J. Anthony Lukas divides the Chicago Conspiracy Trial into five "phases." The first period, which Lukas calls "The Jelly Bean Phase," lasted from September 24 to October 13. It was a relatively uneventful stage, in which the defendants took a "gently mocking" stance toward the trial. The second period, the "Gags and Shackles Phase," lasted from October 14 to November 5. [In this phase the defendants sought] to emphasize political issues in the trial, perhaps because they were concerned that the trial was being seen by their sympathizers as a mere joke. Also during this phase, Black Panther defendant Bobby Seale continuously, and in increasingly angry tones, insisted upon his right either to represent himself or to have the trial continued until his own counsel of choice, Charles Garry [another Black Panther] (who was hospitalized for gall bladder surgery), could represent him. Seale hurled frequent and bitter attacks at Judge Hoffman, calling him a "fascist dog," a "pig," and a "racist," among other things. On October 29, the outraged judge ordered Seale bound and gagged. Finally, on November 5, Hoffman severed Seale from the case and sentenced him to four years in prison for contempt. The Chicago Eight suddenly became the Chicago Seven. Phase three, lasting from November 6 to December 10, was called by Lukas "Government's Day in Court." It was a relatively calm period with only nine contempts, as the defendants saw in a surprisingly weak prosecution case the opportunity for at least a hung jury if they could "cool it" and avoid turning the jury against them. Phase four, from December 11 to January 22 was the "Sing Along with Phil and Judy Phase." This was the phase in which the defense presented its witnesses, a virtual "who's who" of the American left from the guru of the drug culture Timothy Leary to radical poet Allen Ginsberg to folk singers Phil Ochs, Arlo Guthrie, "Country Joe" McDonald, Pete Seeger and Judy Collins. The final phase of the trial, from January 23 to February 7, Lukas called the "Barnyard Epithet Phase." It was a two-week period marked by increasingly bitter outbursts by the defendants and their attorneys, and by almost irrational overreactions by Judge Hoffman. Forty-eight contempts came in this shortest of the five trial phases.

The heart of the government's case was presented through the testimony of three undercover agents who had infiltrated radical ranks, Irwin Bock, William Frappolly, and Robert Pierson. Pierson landed a job as Rubin's "bodyguard," while Bock and Frappolly maneuvered their way into leadership positions in "Vets for Peace" and the SDS (Students for a Democratic Society). The undercover witnesses described plots to disrupt traffic, takeover hotels, "sabotage" restrooms, and other "hit-and-run guerilla tactics." The government's case was aided substantially by Judge Hoffman who consistently ruled in favor of the prosecution on evidentiary disputes. For example, Hoffman allowed the government to introduce speeches of the defendants made well before their arrival in Chicago when they tended to support the government's case, but ruled that the defense could not introduce (because they were "self-serving") pre-Convention documents that suggested peaceable intentions. Throughout the presentation of the government's case, [attorney] Thomas Foran played the straight man, while his younger associate, Richard Shultz, expressed outrage at defense behavior and—whenever the opportunity arose—went for the jugular. J. Anthony Lukas marveled that "Shultz could have made the first robin of spring sound like a plot by the Audobon Society."

The defense through its witnesses tried to portray the defendants as committed idealists who reacted spontaneously to escalating police violence. It suggested that what the prosecution saw as dangerous plots, such as an alleged Yippie conspiracy to place LSD in the Chicago water supply, were only play. The defense also attempted, without much success because of Judge Hoffman's rulings excluding such testimony, to make the Viet Nam War an issue in the trial. The defense countered the prosecution's attempt to prove a conspiracy with evidence that the alleged conspirators never met as a group—and would have agreed upon little if they had. Defense witness Norman Mailer probably made the point best when he said, "Left-wingers are incapable of conspiracy because they're all egomaniacs." Abbie Hoffman made the same point more colorfully when he said, "Conspiracy? Hell, we couldn't agree on lunch."

Handing Out Convictions

The jury had scarcely begun its deliberations in the Chicago Conspiracy Trial when Judge Hoffman began sentencing each of the defendants and the two defense attorneys, William Kunstler and Leonard Weinglass, to lengthy prison terms on 159 specifications for criminal contempt. The specifications ranged from minor acts of disrespect (such as not standing for the judge) to playful acts (such as baring rib cages or blowing kisses to the jury) to insulting or questioning the integrity of the court ("liar," "hypocrite," and "fascist dog"). William Kunstler, who seemingly became a radicalized brother of his clients over the course of the trial, was sentenced by Hoffman to four years and thirteen days in jail. One specification for Kunstler concerned an incident on February 3 when he said "I am going to turn back to my seat with the realization that everything I have learned throughout my life has come to naught, that there is no meaning in this court, there is no law in this court." The Seventh Circuit Court of Appeals later reversed all contempt convictions, ruling that contempt convictions resulting in more than six months in prison require jury trials.

The jury initially split, with eight jurors voting to convict defendants on both the conspiracy and intent to incite riot charges and four jurors voting to acquit on all charges. Foreman Edward Kratzke handed a hung-jury message to the marshal to take to Judge Hoffman. The judge's response: "Keep deliberating!" Juror Kay Richards finally brokered a compromise between the two jury factions. In the end, jurors acquitted all defendants on the conspiracy charge, while finding the five defendants charged with having an intent to incite a riot while crossing state lines guilty. The jury acquitted Froines and Weiner of the charge of teaching and demonstrating the use of an incendiary device.

On February 20, 1970, Judge Hoffman sentenced the five members of the Chicago Seven found guilty by the jury. Each defendant made a statement before sentence was imposed. David Dellinger told Hoffman that he was "a man who had too much power over too many people for too many years," but that he admired his "spunk." Rennie Davis announced that when he got out of prison he intended to "move next door to [prosecutor] Tom Foran, and bring his sons and daughter into the revolution." Tom Hayden offered the opinion that "we would hardly have been notorious characters if they left us alone on the streets of Chicago," but instead "we became the architects, the masterminds, and the geniuses of a conspiracy to overthrow the government—we were invented." Abbie Hoffman recommended that the judge try LSD: "I know a good dealer in Florida [where the judge was soon to head for a vacation]; I could fix you up." Jerry Rubin offered the judge a copy of his new book *Do It!* with an inscription inside: "Julius, you radicalized more young people than we ever could. You're the country's top Yippie." After listening to each defendant give his statement, Judge Hoffman sentenced each defendant to five years' imprisonment plus a $5,000 fine.

Reversing the Convictions

The Seventh Circuit Court of Appeals reversed all convictions on November 21, 1972. The appellate court based its decision on the refusal to allow inquiry into the cultural biases of potential jurors during voir dire as well as Judge Hoffman's "deprecatory and often antagonistic attitude toward the defense." The court also noted that it was determined after appellate argument that the F.B.I., with the knowledge and complicity of Judge Hoffman and prosecutors, had bugged the offices of the Chicago defense attorneys. The Court of Appeals panel said that it had "little doubt but that the wrongdoing of F.B.I. agents would have required reversal of the convictions on the substantive charges."

All seven Chicago police officers charged with violating the civil rights of demonstrators were acquitted. Charges against an eighth officer were dismissed. Richard Shultz explained the verdicts by observing, "The people who sit on juries in this city are just not ready to convict a Chicago policeman."

There is no simple "yes" or "no" answer to the question of whether the Chicago defendants intended to incite a riot in Chicago in 1968. Abbie Hoffman said, "I don't know whether I'm innocent or I'm guilty." The reason for the confusion—as Norman Mailer pointed out—was that the alleged conspirators "understood that you didn't have to attack the fortress anymore." All they had to do was "surround it, make faces at the people inside and let them have nervous breakdowns and destroy themselves."

Millions March in Vietnam Moratorium

By Anthony R. Dolan

The Vietnam Moratorium was the largest demonstration in U.S. history, with approximately 20 million to 30 million people involved. In October American combat troops had been fighting the Communist Vietcong in Vietnam for four years. Some forty-five thousand Americans had been killed, almost half a million U.S. men and women were deployed in the conflict, and opposition to the war was growing. The moratorium for the first time brought out America's middle class and middle-aged voters, in large numbers. In towns and cities throughout the United States, students, working men and women, and school children took part in antiwar religious services, school seminars, street rallies, and meetings. Supporters of the Vietnam Moratorium wore black armbands to signify their dissent and paid tribute to American personnel killed in the war since 1961. The focal point was the capital, Washington, D.C., where more than forty different activities were planned. Some peace demonstrators gathered on the Capitol steps singing songs and holding a candlelit vigil until rallies began in the morning. The enormous crowd heightened political awareness of the growing antiwar sentiment in the United States. In the following article, Anthony R. Dolan recounts the planning and execution of the largest protest in America's history. Dolan is a scholar with the American Enterprise Institute, a conservative political think tank.

Anthony R. Dolan, "Push Button, End War," *National Review*, November 4, 1969. Copyright © 1969 by National Review, Inc. Reproduced by permission.

The Tuesday before the Wednesday [October 15, 1969], Moratorium headquarters in Washington looked chaotic. It was only busy. On the eighth floor of the office building it occupied at Fourteenth and Vermont, the volunteers were stuffing and licking and stamping, working, already, on the mailing for the two-day demonstration planned for November. In his office, Sam Brown, the architect of the Youth for McCarthy crusade[1] and now of the Moratorium, was explaining to a reporter from the *Los Angeles Times* that the protest was not meant to embarrass [President Richard] Nixon but to build him a constituency for the only real goal of the demonstration—immediate American withdrawal from Vietnam. In another office down the hall, David Hawk, the all-American diver from Cornell and another cochairman of the drive, was telling another reporter: "We're trying to get beyond the academic community and into the suburbs. This has basically been a grass-roots movement, all we've done from the national office is coordinate the activities. We're trying to get Americans to put pressure on their elevated officials at the local level. The guts of this thing is really community organizing."

Inside the Moratorium Offices
The walls of the Moratorium offices were decorated with the "Push the Button, End the War" and "Fathers and Sons against the War" posters that once had been full-page ads in the *New York Times*. Also pasted up were the letters from thirteen-year-old girls who'd donated their allowances, as well as the notes of support from servicemen still in Vietnam. There were newspaper clippings too, the ones the office workers found encouraging—"HERSHEY FED TO PROTESTORS": "TOM SEAVER[2] OPPOSES WAR."

Against one of the giant doorbells (the buttons you were supposed to push to end the war), Mary Lou Oates stood that morning, another veteran of the McCarthy campaign and now the press secretary for the Moratorium committee. She was asked by an attentive newsman if this was the movement that began in the "snows of New Hampshire." "It began in Mississippi in '64," was her reply. "But we've been more successful. We've already achieved a victory; we've focused attention back on the war."

---

1. The Youth for McCarthy crusade supported democratic senator Eugene McCarthy's campaign to run for president in 1968. McCarthy lost the nomination as democratic presidential candidate to Hubert Humphrey.   2. Tom Seaver was a professional baseball player for the New York Mets.

Across the room at almost the same moment, John Boyles, who is the other press secretary when he is not the chaplain at Swarthmore, was saying in response to a hostile question: "I haven't given it all that much thought, but I really don't see another Hué,[3] if we pulled out. I'm not at all sure the Vietcong would initiate a bloodbath. Anyway, what do we have now?" And in the main office, amidst the stuffers and the lickers and the stampers, "Bruce-Morton-of-CBS," as he called himself, was telling a camera and a battery of TV lights that the next day's demonstration would probably be the biggest in American history.

He was not wrong: fifty thousand in New Haven, eighty thousand in Boston, two hundred thousand in New York. The reports kept flowing into Moratorium headquarters; the newsmen were kept informed. Students on over a thousand college campuses sponsored voter canvassing efforts, and teach-ins, and readings of the list of war dead. In London, Paul Newman led a march around the American embassy; in New York City, Mayor [John V.] Lindsay told a noontime crowd that America must "recapture her soul"; in Cincinnati, rabbinical students marched around the Federal Building blowing trumpets and waiting for the walls to fall; and in California, at Nixon's alma mater, Whittier College, the students set up a "flame of life," to burn until the war was over. It was not all clockwork. It poured in San Francisco; in Boston, the *Harvard Crimson* printed an embarrassing editorial which read: "It is time to declare we reject not only the methods of American intervention but the goals. The National Liberation Front[4] has the support of the people of Vietnam. It deserves our support as well."

The Youthful Idealist

At the three o'clock briefing, Brown told a roomful of reporters: "Gentlemen, we cannot believe that the President will continue the war in the face of the massive outpouring we're witnessing across the country. A substantial percentage, if not the majority, of the American people oppose the continuation of this war." But when the questions began, Brown was asked by two persistent reporters to renounce, once and for all, the support of both Hanoi and do-

3. Hué was the scene of the longest and heaviest fighting of the Vietnam War. Some 4,000 civilians were killed, and most of the city, including ancient palaces and tombs, were destroyed.   4. The National Liberation Front (NLF) is a title used by nationalist, usually socialist, movements in various countries since World War II. In Vietnam, the National Front for the Liberation of the South (the Vietcong) was formed in 1960 to overthrow the South Vietnamese government.

mestic Communists as well. Brown's eyes blazed; he refused to meet the challenge. He seemed, at that moment, the picture of the youthful idealist, reacting angrily to the questions he thought so plainly unfair. It was easy to admire him; it was difficult to remember he was a thoroughly experienced, professional politician.

Even so, Mary McGrory, a Brown admirer, reported the next day that the questions had "rattled" Brown. Brown's reaction at the briefing was actually reflective of the counterprotest the Moratorium aroused. On the day of the demonstrations, the Citizens Committee for Peace with Security placed full-page "TELL IT TO HANOI" ads in many newspapers, while the Committee for Responsible Patriotism urged those who disagreed with the protestors to drive with their headlights on. In Washington, after dissenting students had walked out, Congressman Buz Lukens told a cheering high-school audience, "I am not a defensive American. I am, by God, proud of my country." In New York, despite Mayor Lindsay's directive, the flag stayed at full staff at Shea Stadium during the World Series game. Later Lindsay was to apologize for his order that City flags be flown at half-staff. In Philadelphia, the city buses were decorated with patriotic colors; while at Cape Kennedy hundreds of workers drove to their jobs with their headlights on.

A Substantial Response

And though the demonstrations inspired the usual run of "Youth-with-the-Truth" articles, though "Bruce-Morton-of-CBS" managed to sound properly enthusiastic, some segments of the media were curiously unbiased. Not a few people groaned in Moratorium headquarters when, for instance, David Brinkley described the public response as "substantial but not enormous." At the end of the telecast, Sam Brown was overheard complaining, "They showed only kids. They showed all the counterprotest, as if it's even. They didn't give crowd figures."

Even Mrs. [Martin Luther] King's speech at the Washington Monument, delivered in those slow deliberate tones reminiscent of her husband's speaking style, and the candlelight march she led around the White House had their impact somewhat dulled by the news that Henry Kissinger[5] was, at the time, sitting in the White

5. Henry Kissinger was a political scientist, who, as adviser for national security affairs and secretary of state, was a major influence in the shaping of foreign policy from 1969 to 1976.

House basement reading by himself while the President was upstairs alone in his office working on his Latin American policy.

But it may well have been Tuesday evening's abortive all-night House session that best indicated the success the Moratorium enjoyed, as well as the elements of counter-protest it aroused. The doves in the House had planned an antiwar gangbang lasting through the night, but the Republican leadership managed to put together enough votes for adjournment.

Outside, the students had gathered on the center steps at the east front of the Capitol. They were singing "Where Have All the Flowers Gone," "Blowin' in the Wind" and the other peace songs. One of them, whose hair was not that long, periodically led the "Give me a P" cheer and ended it always with a wave of his arms as the crowd chanted, faster and faster, "Peace Now/Peace Now/Peace Now." The weather was brisk enough, but not really cold. The wind was easily heard in the trees. The girls were pretty too. It was autumn, but those who looked instinctively for the cheerleaders did so in vain.

Speaking to the Students

[Congressman] James Scheuer from New York spoke to the students. He told them: "I hope and pray the President will be sensitive to the consensus that's going to roar across the country tomorrow from Maine to California." From behind the Congressman, you could see, through the TV lights, the line of Capitol policemen at the top of the steps and beneath them the students cheering. Over Scheuer's voice and the applause, you could also hear another sound. Sometimes, over the heads of the policemen and the demonstrators, just before your eyes began their sweep up the great lighted dome, you could see the flag, whipping and cracking, distressedly, in the wind.

President Nixon Announces the Vietnamization Plan

By Richard Nixon

Soon after taking office, President Richard Nixon introduced his policy of "Vietnamization." The plan was to encourage the South Vietnamese to take more responsibility for fighting the war. It was hoped that this policy would eventually enable the United States to withdraw gradually from Vietnam and save face over a war that many thought the United States was losing. In June, Nixon announced the first of the U.S. troop withdrawals in response to the program. The 540,000 U.S. troops were to be reduced by 25,000. Another 60,000 were to leave the following December. To increase the size of the Army of the Republic of Vietnam, a mobilization law was passed that called up into the army all men in South Vietnam aged between seventeen and forty-three.

Despite the Vietnamization plan, the United States continued to drop bombs on the North Vietnamese enemy, and U.S. soldiers continued to die. U.S. troops remained in Vietnam until the end of the war in 1973. The following article is excerpted from a speech given by Nixon in November 1969 that explains the details of his Vietnamization plan.

Good evening, my fellow Americans: Tonight I want to talk to you on a subject of deep concern to all Americans and to many people in all parts of the world—the war in Vietnam.

Richard Nixon, address to the nation, Washington, DC, November 3, 1969.

I believe that one of the reasons for the deep division about Vietnam is that many Americans have lost confidence in what their Government has told them about our policy. The American people cannot and should not be asked to support a policy which involves the overriding issues of war and peace unless they know the truth about that policy.

Tonight, therefore, I would like to answer some of the questions that I know are on the minds of many of you listening to me:

• How and why did America get involved in Vietnam in the first place?

• How has this administration changed the policy of the previous administration?

• What has really happened in the negotiations in Paris and on the battlefront in Vietnam?

• What choices do we have if we are to end the war?

• What are the prospects for peace?

The War Situation

Now, let me begin by describing the situation I found when I was inaugurated on January 20 [1969].

• The war had been going on for 4 years.

• 31,000 Americans had been killed in action.

• The training program for the South Vietnamese was behind schedule.

• 540,000 Americans were in Vietnam with no plans to reduce the number.

• No progress had been made at the negotiations in Paris and the United States had not put forth a comprehensive peace proposal.

• The war was causing deep division at home and criticism from many of our friends as well as our enemies abroad. . . .

The Fundamental Issue

Well, let us turn now to the fundamental issue. Why and how did the United States become involved in Vietnam in the first place?

Fifteen years ago North Vietnam, with the logistical support of Communist China and the Soviet Union, launched a campaign to impose a Communist government on South Vietnam by instigating and supporting a revolution.

In response to the request of the Government of South Vietnam, President [Dwight D.] Eisenhower sent economic aid and military equipment to assist the people of South Vietnam in their efforts to prevent a Communist takeover. Seven years ago, President [John F.] Kennedy sent 16,000 military personnel to Vietnam as combat advisers.

Four years ago, President [Lyndon B.] Johnson sent American combat forces to South Vietnam.

Now, many believe that President Johnson's decision to send American combat forces to South Vietnam was wrong. And many others—I among them—have been strongly critical of the way the war has been conducted.

But the question facing us today is: Now that we are in the war, what is the best way to end it?

In January I could only conclude that the precipitate withdrawal of American forces from Vietnam would be a disaster not only for South Vietnam but for the United States and for the cause of peace.

For the South Vietnamese, our precipitate withdrawal would inevitably allow the Communists to repeat the massacres which followed their takeover in the North 15 years before.

• They then murdered more than 50,000 people and hundreds of thousands more died in slave labor camps.

• We saw a prelude of what would happen in South Vietnam when the Communists entered the city of Hue [in 1968]. During their brief rule there, there was a bloody reign of terror in which 3,000 civilians were clubbed, shot to death, and buried in mass graves.

• With the sudden collapse of our support, these atrocities of Hue would become the nightmare of the entire nation—and particularly for the million and a half Catholic refugees who fled to South Vietnam when the Communists took over in the North.

For the United States, this first defeat in our Nation's history would result in a collapse of confidence in American leadership, not only in Asia but throughout the world. . . .

For the future of peace, precipitate withdrawal would thus be a disaster of immense magnitude.

• A nation cannot remain great if it betrays its allies and lets down its friends.

• Our defeat and humiliation in South Vietnam without question would promote recklessness in the councils of those great powers who have not yet abandoned their goals of world conquest.

• This would spark violence wherever our commitments help maintain the peace—in the Middle East, in Berlin, eventually even in the Western Hemisphere.

Ultimately, this would cost more lives.

It would not bring peace; it would bring more war.

For these reasons, I rejected the recommendation that I should end the war by immediately withdrawing all of our forces. I chose instead to change American policy on both the negotiating front and battlefront.

A Pursuit for Peace

In order to end a war fought on many fronts, I initiated a pursuit for peace on many fronts.

In a television speech on May 14, in a speech before the United Nations, and on a number of other occasions I set forth our peace proposals in great detail.

• We have offered the complete withdrawal of all outside forces within 1 year.

• We have proposed a cease-fire under international supervision.

• We have offered free elections under international supervision with the Communists participating in the organization and conduct of the elections as an organized political force. And the Saigon Government has pledged to accept the result of the elections.

We have not put forth our proposals on a take-it-or-leave-it basis. We have indicated that we are willing to discuss the proposals that have been put forth by the other side. We have declared that anything is negotiable except the right of the people of South Vietnam to determine their own future. At the Paris peace conference, Ambassador [John Davis] Lodge has demonstrated our flexibility and good faith in 40 public meetings.

Hanoi has refused even to discuss our proposals. They demand our unconditional acceptance of their terms, which are that we withdraw all American forces immediately and unconditionally and that we overthrow the Government of South Vietnam as we leave.

We have not limited our peace initiatives to public forums and public statements. I recognized, in January, that a long and bitter war like this usually cannot be settled in a public forum. That is why in addition to the public statements and negotiations I have explored every possible private avenue that might lead to a settlement.

Public Disclosure

Tonight I am taking the unprecedented step of disclosing to you some of our other initiatives for peace—initiatives we undertook privately and secretly because we thought we thereby might open

President Richard Nixon meets with American soldiers in Vietnam in 1969. The goal of Nixon's Vietnamization plan was for the United States to gradually withdraw its troops from the war.

a door which publicly would be closed. I did not wait for my inauguration to begin my quest for peace.

• Soon after my election, through an individual who is directly in contact on a personal basis with the leaders of North Vietnam, I made two private offers for a rapid, comprehensive settlement. Hanoi's replies called in effect for our surrender before negotiations.

• Since the Soviet Union furnishes most of the military equipment for North Vietnam, Secretary of State [William] Rogers, my Assistant for National Security Affairs, Dr. [Henry] Kissinger, Ambassador Lodge, and I, personally, have met on a number of occasions with representatives of the Soviet Government to enlist their assistance in getting meaningful negotiations started. In addition, we have had extended discussions directed toward that same end with representatives of other governments which have diplomatic relations with North Vietnam. None of these initiatives have to date produced results.

• In mid-July, I became convinced that it was necessary to make a major move to break the deadlock in the Paris talks. I spoke directly in this office, where I am now sitting, with an individual who had known Ho Chi Minh [president, Democratic Republic of Vietnam] on a personal basis for 25 years.

Through him I sent a letter to Ho Chi Minh.

I did this outside of the usual diplomatic channels with the hope that with the necessity of making statements for propaganda removed, there might be constructive progress toward bringing the war to an end. . . .

I received Ho Chi Minh's reply on August 30 [1969], 3 days before his death. It simply reiterated the public position North Vietnam had taken at Paris and flatly rejected my initiative. . . .

But the effect of all the public, private, and secret negotiations which have been undertaken since the bombing halt a year ago and since this administration came into office on January 20, can be summed up in one sentence: No progress whatever has been made except agreement on the shape of the bargaining table.

Well now, who is at fault?

It has become clear that the obstacle in negotiating an end to the war is not the President of the United States. It is not the South Vietnamese Government.

The obstacle is the other side's absolute refusal to show the least willingness to join us in seeking a just peace. And it will not do so while it is convinced that all it has to do is to wait for our next concession, and our next concession after that one, until it gets everything it wants.

There can now be no longer any question that progress in negotiation depends only on Hanoi's deciding to negotiate, to negotiate seriously.

I realize that this report on our efforts on the diplomatic front is discouraging to the American people, but the American people are entitled to know the truth—the bad news as well as the good news—where the lives of our young men are involved.

The Nixon Doctrine

Now let me turn, however, to a more encouraging report on another front.

At the time we launched our search for peace I recognized we might not succeed in bringing an end to the war through negotiation. I, therefore, put into effect another plan to bring peace—a plan which will bring the war to an end regardless of what happens on the negotiating front.

It is in line with a major shift in U.S. foreign policy which I described in my press conference at Guam on July 25. Let me briefly explain what has been described as the Nixon Doctrine—a policy which not only will help end the war in Vietnam, but which is an essential element of our program to prevent future Vietnams.

We Americans are a do-it-yourself people. We are an impatient people. Instead of teaching someone else to do a job, we like to do it ourselves. And this trait has been carried over into our foreign policy.

In Korea and again in Vietnam, the United States furnished most of the money, most of the arms, and most of the men to help the people of those countries defend their freedom against Communist aggression.

Before any American troops were committed to Vietnam, a leader of another Asian country expressed this opinion to me when I was traveling in Asia as a private citizen. He said: "When you are trying to assist another nation defend its freedom, U.S. policy should be to help them fight the war but not to fight the war for them."

Well, in accordance with this wise counsel, I laid down in Guam three principles as guidelines for future American policy toward Asia:

• First, the United States will keep all of its treaty commitments.

• Second, we shall provide a shield if a nuclear power threatens the freedom of a nation allied with us or of a nation whose survival we consider vital to our security.

• Third, in cases involving other types of aggression, we shall furnish military and economic assistance when requested in accordance with our treaty commitments. But we shall look to the nation directly threatened to assume the primary responsibility of providing the manpower for its defense.

After I announced this policy, I found that the leaders of the Philippines, Thailand, Vietnam, South Korea, and other nations which might be threatened by Communist aggression, welcomed this new direction in American foreign policy.

The defense of freedom is everybody's business not just America's business. And it is particularly the responsibility of the people whose freedom is threatened.

Vietnamizing the Search for Peace

In the previous administration, we Americanized the war in Vietnam. In this administration, we are Vietnamizing the search for peace.

The policy of the previous administration not only resulted in our assuming the primary responsibility for fighting the war, but even more significantly did not adequately stress the goal of strengthening the South Vietnamese so that they could defend themselves when we left.

The Vietnamization plan was launched following Secretary [Melvin R.] Laird's visit to Vietnam in March [1969]. Under the plan, I ordered first a substantial increase in the training and equipment of South Vietnamese forces.

In July, on my visit to Vietnam, I changed General [Creighton W.] Abrams' orders so that they were consistent with the objectives of our new policies. Under the new orders, the primary mission of our troops is to enable the South Vietnamese forces to assume the full responsibility for the security of South Vietnam.

Our air operations have been reduced by over 20 percent.

And now we have begun to see the results of this long overdue change in American policy in Vietnam.

• After 5 years of Americans going into Vietnam, we are finally bringing American men home. By December 15 [1969], over 60,000 men will have been withdrawn from South Vietnam—including 20 percent of all of our combat forces.

• The South Vietnamese have continued to gain in strength. As a result they have been able to take over combat responsibilities from our American troops. . . .

We have adopted a plan which we have worked out in cooperation with the South Vietnamese for the complete withdrawal of all U.S. combat ground forces, and their replacement by South Vietnamese forces on an orderly scheduled timetable. This withdrawal will be made from strength and not from weakness. As South Vietnamese forces become stronger, the rate of American withdrawal can become greater. . . .

A Statement of Policy

Hanoi could make no greater mistake than to assume that an increase in violence will be to its advantage. If I conclude that increased enemy action jeopardizes our remaining forces in Vietnam, I shall not hesitate to take strong and effective measures to deal with that situation.

This is not a threat. This is a statement of policy, which as Commander in Chief of our Armed Forces, I am making in meeting my responsibility for the protection of American fighting men wherever they may be.

My fellow Americans, I am sure you can recognize from what I have said that we really only have two choices open to us if we want to end this war.

• I can order an immediate, precipitate withdrawal of all Americans from Vietnam without regard to the effects of that action.

• Or we can persist in our search for a just peace through a negotiated settlement if possible, or through continued implementation of our plan for Vietnamization if necessary—a plan in which we will withdraw all of our forces from Vietnam on a schedule in accordance with our program, as the South Vietnamese become strong enough to defend their own freedom.

I have chosen this second course.

It is not the easy way.

It is the right way.

It is a plan which will end the war and serve the cause of peace—not just in Vietnam but in the Pacific and in the world. . . .

Thank you and goodnight.

Paul McCartney Is Rumored to Be Dead

By John Neary

In 1969 a rumor circulated that Paul McCartney, a member of one of the most influential and popular rock bands in history, the Beatles, had died in a car accident. In the following article, John Neary, contributor to *Life* magazine in 1969, examines the rumor and offers reputed evidence of McCartney's death, including bizarre album covers and hidden tracks in records. However, Neary also includes a statement by McCartney that clearly affirms his existence and refutes allegations of his death. The "Paul is dead" rumor is one of the most controversial debates in music history, and some people still claim that the "original" Paul McCartney died in 1966 and was replaced by a look-alike.

With an apparent superabundance of clues solidly in hand and firmly on the record, the mere fact that the subject of one of the most intensive manhunts in recent history modestly declared that he, himself, had not yet learned of his death cast hardly a pall on the exhilaration of the chase.

Thousands and thousands of distraught Beatle fans were anxiously weighing the "evidence" and concluding that some mishap had befallen Beatle Paul McCartney. He had died. Or something. They figured.

The Evidence

There was plenty to go on. Investigators had spent hours . . .
studying Beatle record album jackets with the meticulous
scrutiny of CIA photo-interpreters microscoping aerials of enemy missile sites. They had spiraled down the grooves of every
Beatle record ever cut, speeding them up from 33 to 45 rpm, to
78, slowing them to 16—even taping them and then reversing
the tapes, analyzing stereo recordings track by track. There could
be no doubt about it, they concluded. "I mean, it's all right there,"
pronounced Louis Yager, president of the Is Paul McCartney
Dead Society at Hofstra University.

On the album jackets there appeared to be a welter of per-
plexing symbols, ranging from the hand over Paul's head on the
Sgt. Pepper cover to such oddments as the walrus costume on
Magical Mystery Tour, the black carnation Paul wears in the
same album (the other Beatles are wearing red ones), the funeral
procession that is on the back of *Abbey Road* and the photo inside the *Mystery Tour* album, where Paul sits in military uniform,
above a large sign stating, "I was."

This all seemed somewhat circumstantial, even conjectural,
but buttressing the findings was some startling aural evidence.
Deep down in the grooves at the very end of the song *Strawberry
Fields*, on the *Magical Mystery Tour* album, investigators had
discovered a voice eerily like John Lennon's saying, "I buried
Paul." It was even clearer at 45 rpm. Then, in what is called the
"white" album—the one labeled simply *The Beatles*—there is a
nine-minute montage of sounds, *Revolution No. 9*. In it a man's
voice intones repeatedly, "Number nine, number nine." McCartney's name has nine letters in it. Moreover, if this intonation is
taped and then played in reverse, a quite different voice will be
heard to say, "Turn me on, dead man, turn me on, dead man."

Then, if the whole band of *Revolution No. 9* is reversed, the
horrifying sounds of a traffic accident, a bad one, too, emerge: a
collision, crackling flames, a voice crying, "Get me out, get me
out?" If the piece is taped *stereophonically* and then *reversed*,
this is what is heard on one of the four tracks: "He hit a pole! We
better get him to see a surgeon. [Scream.] So anyhow, he went
to see a dentist instead. They gave him a pair of teeth that weren't
any good at all so—[A car horn blares.] My wings are broken
and so is my hair. I'm not in the mood for words. [Gurgling, bat-

tle sounds.] Find the night watchman. A fine natural imbalance. Must have got it in the shoulder blades."

Empty Tracks

Not even the ordinarily blank grooves between the song bands escaped scrutiny. In one such "empty" track, on side two of the white album, between *I'm So Tired* and *Blackbird*, a sleuth over at radio station WNEW in New York discovered some moaning. When the moaning is reversed, one can hear John Lennon declaring, "Paul is dead. Miss him. Miss him. Miss him."

Finally, of course, a large number of investigators went right to the core of the conundrum and called the Beatles' firm in London, Apple, Ltd. There, a flabbergasted Derek Taylor, the Beatles' agent, released a statement from Paul. He was, Taylor said, off in the country with his family, but he had sent word back that "If I were dead, I'd be the last to know." That sounded reassuringly like the old Paul. As for the voice in *Strawberry Fields*, claims Taylor, it is saying, "I'm very bored," not "I buried Paul." That was as far as Taylor would go. The Beatles didn't expect people to go around reversing their records. He did admit that

The Beatles perform onstage in 1967. Two years later a rumor began circulating that Paul McCartney had died and had been replaced with a look-alike.

putting stuff in there in reverse was just the sort of something that sly John Lennon might have done.

Ringo, called into consultation, was brisk. "It's a load of old crap," he said. Anyway, Ringo said, it was John Lennon, not Paul, wearing the walrus suit.

Investigators were not convinced. The lyrics of Paul's own songs furnish other deadly clues. On *Revolver*, Paul sings, "I was alone, I took a ride, I didn't know what I would find there, another road . . ." And in *A Day in the Life* he refers to a man who "blew his mind out in a car." Surely these are additional references to a fatal car accident! Noting a license plate on the Volkswagen in the *Abbey Road* cover, Louis Yager placed an overseas call to that number in London, awakening an elderly lady who, in terms somewhat like Ringo's, declined comment. Undaunted, Yager and his group reevaluated their investigation. "We originally thought he was dead. But we decided that was too emotional. We all ought to sit back and analyze this rationally."

In Paul's Words

Meantime, Paul McCartney himself delivered his own analysis. It is all bloody stupid. I picked up that O.P.D. badge in Canada. It was a police badge. Perhaps it means Ontario Police Department or something. I was wearing a black flower because they ran out of red ones. It is John, not me, dressed in black on the cover and inside of *Magical Mystery Tour.* On *Abbey Road* we were wearing our ordinary clothes. I was walking barefoot because it was a hot day. The Volkswagen just happened to be parked there.

Perhaps the rumor started because I haven't been much in the press lately. I have done enough press for a lifetime and I don't have anything to say these days. I am happy to be with my family and I will work when I work. I was switched on for 10 years and I never switched off. Now I am switching off whenever I can. I would rather be a little less famous these days.

I would rather do what I began by doing, which was making music. We make good music and we want to go on making good music. But the Beatle thing is over. It has been exploded, partly by what we have done and partly by other people. We are individuals, all different. John married Yoko, I married Linda. We didn't marry the same girl. The people who are making up these rumors should look to themselves a little more. There is not enough time in life. They should worry about themselves instead of worrying whether I am dead or not.

What I have to say is all in the music. If I want to say anything I write a song. Can you spread it around that I am just an ordinary person and want to live in peace? We have to go now, we have two children at home.

Native Americans Occupy Alcatraz

By John A. Coleman

In November 1969 approximately one hundred Native American students occupied Alcatraz island in San Francisco. They demanded that the U.S. government cede the land to the Native Americans, and they wanted to establish a Native American university, a cultural center, and a museum on the island. They immediately organized an elected council, and everyone on the island had a job: security, sanitation, day care, school, housing, cooking, and laundry. In addition, all decisions were made by unanimous consent of the people.

The federal government initially responded by insisting that the Indian people leave Alcatraz and by placing a barricade around the island. However, they eventually agreed to demands by the Indian council that formal negotiations be held. The government refused to grant the Indians' demands despite the fact that some of the tribespeople remained on Alcatraz until 1971. In June of that year, federal marshals forcibly removed the remaining Native Americans from the island. In the following article, John A. Coleman recounts the events of the occupation and celebrates the Native Americans' attempt to redress some of the wrongs wrought by the United States throughout history. At the time the following article was published, Coleman was a fellow with the Department of Sociology at the University of California, Berkeley.

We had been led to expect the worst. Columnist Herb Caen had proclaimed a week earlier in the San Francisco *Chronicle* that they were like the band from *Lord of the Flies*—young, savage, forgetful of the long lessons of civilization and the price we pay to forge order out of chaos.

As we waited on the dock, the island fortress was barely visible in the morning rain. Five of us were "gentiles," the others native American Indians. On the trip across the bay I let my fantasy play, imagining that I was a federal prisoner leaving the mainland for a life-time exile on "the rock." I shuddered as the fantasy became too real.

The Fear Inside You

The wife of a television cameraman was clearly skittish. "Aren't you afraid to sleep over there—I mean with all those men?" she asked a pretty, blond college girl who came on the boat with her sleeping bag. She pressed the college co-ed with several more questions, each containing the underlying theme of fear. Finally, the young girl replied: "I'm not afraid. Why should I be? They are my people. Besides, fear is inside you. It is there that you must conquer it. That is what we are trying to do." Later I learned that this young girl, the granddaughter of Jim Thorpe, had come down from school in Portland to help her people conquer the one fear that counts, the fear inside you.

As we approached Alcatraz, signs awaited us, proclaiming: "Indians Welcome," "Peace and Brotherhood to Indians of All Tribes." A Pima Indian soldier from Fort Ord who had come to the island in search of his uncle nudged me, pointed to the sign which said: "'Indians Welcome.' Where have you ever seen that before? I've been all over this country. This is the first time I ever saw a sign saying welcome to any Indian. Makes you feel good."

We were met on the dock by a disciplined group of young adults with bands on their arms stating that they were security police of Alcatraz. Instead of *Lord of the Flies* chaos, the island and its population seemed orderly, constructive, brimming with enthusiastic purpose.

The First Invasion

The first invasion of the island had occurred several months earlier, November 14, 1969. Fourteen college students from the Bay Area—most of them veterans of the Third World Student Movement at Berkeley and San Francisco State—landed on Alcatraz with a few blankets, three cans of beer and some sandwiches. La Nada Means, one of these original invaders, told of her purpose in undertaking the invasion of the island.

"We're going to make the plans for our life rather than let someone else do it for us." The students issued a proclamation to the Great White Father and all his people in which they stated their purpose in reclaiming the land known as Alcatraz Island in the name of all American Indians throughout the country.

The rhetoric of the initial proclamation shows a mastery of irony. "We will purchase said Alcatraz Island for twenty-four dollars (24) in glass beads and red cloth, a precedent set by the white man's purchase of a similar island about 300 years ago." The document goes on to point out that the Indian offer of $1.24 per acre is greater than the 47¢ per acre the white men are now paying the California Indians for their land.

The local press treated the initial invasion as a publicity stunt, the prank of college students providing a human interest slant on the news. Six days later, however, a more serious invasion of the island took place. This time 89 men, women and children arrived with the clear intention of staying on the rock.

Swelling Ranks

For about a day the Coast Guard blockaded the island in an effort to stop boats from landing with food and provisions. This blockade aroused public indignation and sympathy for the Indians. By Thanksgiving Day, 700 Indians swelled the population of the little island in the bay.

The "Question Man" in the San Francisco *Chronicle* asked his respondents whether they favored Indian occupation of Alcatraz. "Why not let them have the island?" most reasoned. "What is it good for, anyway?" Alcatraz had stood abandoned since 1963, when the last of the federal prisoners were removed.

Subsequently, the City of San Francisco entered into negotiations with the federal government to purchase the island. The San Francisco Board of Supervisors approved leasing Alcatraz to Texas oil millionaire Lamar Hunt, who planned tourist concessions centering around an astrodome celebrating the U.S. space program. Many Bay Area residents were openly critical of Hunt's scheme, which seemed to them an importation of plastic, tacky America to their beautiful bay. Malvina Reynolds caught this mood in her song about the Indian invasion of Alcatraz: "Alcatraz, who needs that plastic jazz, when the Indians have their way. Who wants an astrodome in San Francisco Bay?"

Why Alcatraz? The choice of the former federal prison was strategic. The Indians state that Alcatraz is more than suitable for an Indian reservation, even when judged by the white man's own standards. They say it resembles most Indian reservations in that: 1) it is isolated from modern facilities, without adequate means of transportation; 2) it has no fresh running water; 3) it has inadequate sanitation facilities; 4) there are no oil or mineral rights; 5) there is no industry and so unemployment is very great; 6) there are no health care facilities; 7) the soil is rocky and nonproductive and the land does not support game; 8) there are no educational facilities; 9) the inhabitants have always exceded the land base; 10) the inhabitants have always been held prisoners and kept dependent upon others.

Accustomed to Hardship

Throughout a day of interviewing residents of the island about hardships and lack of facilities, the invariable answer I received was: "We are used to it. We have lived in worse condtions on our reservations." Typical was the reply of a 23-year-old student: "I'm not a romantic. Hardships are not new to our people. We are used to not having water, electricity or employment. We are used to a high death rate." Many who felt reservation life resembled a prison pointed to the symbolic suitability of choosing a prison for the first Indian invasion in modern times.

What do the Indians plan to do with Alcatraz? Their goal has both short-range and long-range objectives. In the short run, the Indians hope to obtain title to the island and to provide adequate educational, health and food facilities for a resident population of 150. A week earlier than my arrival in the beginning of March [1970], the Indian leaders had sat in conference with federal officials—ending this pow-wow with the traditional smoke of peace. Besides title to the island, the Indian Council of Alcatraz asked $300,000 for planning and study of long-range Indian use of the island. The Indian officials brimmed with optimism about their meeting. They received encouragement from Robert Robertson of the Government Opportunities Commission. It is clear that they expect that the federal government will accede to their demands for ownership of Alcatraz.

Plans for the Island

I talked to John Trudell, 23-year-old former student at Valley College, San Bernardino, California, about long-range use of the island facilities. John, a serious, intelligent Sioux, has been a resident of Alcatraz since November 29 [1969]. He is the announcer on Radio Free Alcatraz, beamed every day from 7:15 to 7:45 P.M. over Berkeley's radio station KPFA. As one of the seven elected members of the island council, he had met a week previously with the representatives of the federal government.

John spoke of the Alcatraz complex becoming an educational center for native American studies. Several Indian institutions are in the planning stage: a Free Indian University with traveling representatives who will visit the reservations; a Museum of Native American History containing archives of documents relating to the history of the American Indian; an American Indian Spiritual Center; an Indian Training School for Crafts; an Indian Center for Ecology. John particularly underscored this last. "If no one else wants to take care of the land, we do. We want our land to survive." In this, John echoed the words of Oneida poet Jerry Hill, who proclaims: "What Earth Mother and Spirit Father have given you, you must develop and return to the life that we are all part of and will return to."

We were given a guided tour of the entire island. The old cell building was particularly depressing. We stopped to note Al Capone's cell and the double cell of the Bird Man of Alcatraz. Until March [1970], the Indians used this old cell building for a mess hall. Recently, however, they have abandoned the building. As Public Relations Director Grace Thorpe put it: "It was just too gloomy walking past all those cell blocks to dinner every day."

The Setup

The 150 Indians live on the northeast corner of the island in what were formerly guards' quarters. There, besides living quarters, a common mess hall and a meeting room, they have set up a health clinic and a one-room school. The school, covering grades one to seven, operates daily, staffed by four certified teachers. The island council has entered into negotiations with the state of California to obtain its accreditation.

I sat for about an hour in the school room, which had formerly served as a chapel for the guards and their families. Books and other provisions were in short supply. I talked to a ten-year-old

Paiute Indian girl, who, with some coaxing, overcame her natural shyness. She had come to the island from Oakland with her mother and brothers on Thanksgiving and stayed ever since. Although she was not quite sure what kind of Indian she was, she was certain she was an Indian and that this was a good thing. She clearly preferred Alcatraz to Oakland.

"What do you learn about Indians in school?" I asked her. In reply, she described ancient stories and songs she had learned and showed me a sample of bead work her class had been taught. As I listened, I recalled the remarks of several college-age Indians who had been sharply critical of the Bureau of Indian Affairs' schools on three counts. They claimed that B.I.A. schools neglected to teach Indian culture and folklore. They were white man's schools. Secondly, they resented the ways B.I.A. schools separated Indian children from their families. One girl described how she had run away from B.I.A. boarding schools three times in order to return to her family in South Dakota. Finally, they claimed that B.I.A. schools prepared students inadequately for college.

I am not competent to assess the truth of their criticism of the Bureau of Indian Affairs' schools. It was unclear to me, also, whether the Alcatraz school did a better or worse job than B.I.A. schools in providing quality preparation for further education. What was apparent was that on Alcatraz an effort is being made to inculcate Indian crafts and folklore without separating the children from their families.

The Sacred Teepee

Near the main buildings there is an overcrowded and makeshift gymnasium where about 20 teen-agers were playing basketball. Directly west of the living compound is a sacred teepee and sweat house, the details of which were supervised by Chief Eagle Feather, a Sioux Indian medicine man from Pine Ridge, S.D. Chief Eagle Feather journeyed to Alcatraz early in February to report a vision he had had about a rocky island in the west to which Indians of all tribes would come and build an intertribal unity that would be the beginning of a great Indian renascence. On this island of his vision there were beautiful purple flowers. By coincidence, the only flower that grows on Alcatraz is a purple geranium. While on Alcatraz Chief Eagle Feather instructed three young island Indians in the ancient arts of the Sun Dance and the Sioux ceremony of the sweat house. We "gentiles" could not set foot on the sacred compound. It is holy ground.

What have the Indians achieved by their occupation of Alcatraz? At best, the island is today only a symbol of hope. Its population depends on good will offerings of food, clothing and medicine to survive. The Indians have yet to receive title to the island and funding for their Indian educational complex. Already, however, by becoming Lords of the Rock, the Indians of Alcatraz have served as a rallying call for unaccustomed intertribal unity. Their motto is a new catch slogan in American Indian history: "Indians of All Tribes."

Already this rallying call has been heard beyond Alcatraz. Since November [1969] an estimated 13,000 Indians have visited Alcatraz from the Pacific Northwest, Arizona, New Mexico and from as far away as Chicago, Minneapolis and Canada. If they talked to the same students I did, they would have heard a new Indian motif: "militant nonviolence." On December 23 [1969], the historic first Indians of All Tribes National Conference was held on Alcatraz, drawing representatives from all parts of the country. The Navajo tribes in Arizona have asked the Alcatraz Indians to provide "Indian runners" to take the message of Alcatraz to Indians on reservations throughout America. The day I visited Alcatraz a delegation of Indians from Pyramid Lake, Nevada, had come to the island to elicit support in their fight with the government to stop encroachment on their water rights by white farmers near Fallon, Nevada, who are siphoning off the Indian water.

On January 31, 1970, in response to a government request to meet with Indian leaders in the Bay Area, the Bay Area Native American Council (BANAC) was formed, representing over 20 Bay Area Indian Organizations, which, in turn, represent 40,000 Indians in the San Francisco region. BANAC is the first intertribal united front in the Bay Area in the wake of the Alcatraz invasion. In their meeting with federal representatives on February 11 [1970], the BANAC leaders echoed the newfound spirit of Alcatraz Indian unity when they said: "BANAC will go on record as supporting the Alcatraz movement by suspending any negotiations with other Indian organizations in the Bay Area now in progress with the federal government until the government recognizes the Alcatraz budget and their program proposal is funded."

In the movie *Tell Them Willie Boy Is Here*, Katherine Ross turns to Robert Perry, who is being chased by a white posse, and says: "You don't have a chance Willie Boy. They are going to kill you." Perry nods in agreement, but adds: "At least they will know Willie Boy was here!" As I write this, it is a clear day over San Francisco Bay. I can see the fortress rock of Alcatraz from my window. Perhaps, in the last analysis, Indian occupation of Alcatraz is only a symbolic gesture, a call to conscience and recognition of the sorry state of the American Indian. Perhaps Katherine Ross is right—they don't have a chance. Nevertheless, today, as on the day I looked back to the rock from the boat at the faces of the Indian children who had come to the dock to wave goodby, I feel glad that they are making us know Willie Boy is there.

The Story of the My Lai Massacre Breaks

By David L. Anderson

On March 16, 1968, a unit of the U.S. Army, led by Lieutenant William L. Calley, invaded the South Vietnamese hamlet of My Lai, an alleged Vietcong stronghold. Calley's unit raped, tortured, and killed 504 unarmed civilians, including children. The incident remained unknown to the American public until the autumn of 1969, when a series of letters by a former soldier, Ron Ridenhour, to government officials forced the army to take action. Several soldiers and veterans were charged with murder, and a number of officers were accused of dereliction of duty for covering up the incident. Special investigations by the U.S. Army and the House of Representatives concluded that a massacre had in fact taken place. Of the many soldiers originally charged, only five were court-martialed, and one, Lieutenant Calley, convicted. Calley served only three years house arrest in retribution for the massacre. The following article is excerpted from David L. Anderson's anthology *Facing My Lai: Moving Beyond the Massacre*. David L. Anderson is professor of history and interim dean of arts and sciences at the University of Indianapolis. He is also the author of *Trapped by Success: The Eisenhower Administration and Vietnam, 1953–1961*.

In November 1969 the American public first learned from brief newspaper reports that U.S. army lieutenant William L. Calley had been charged with multiple murders of Vietnamese civilians at a place called My Lai. At that time, there were about five hundred thousand U.S. troops in Vietnam. American combat units had been there for almost five years, and over forty thousand Americans had been killed in action. The Vietnam War had been the principal issue in the 1968 election that brought Richard Nixon to the White House with a promise to find an honorable way to end the war. The public was tired of and disillusioned with the conflict, and news that U.S. soldiers might be murderers seemed additional evidence of the liability that the war had become. After a military court-martial found Calley guilty in April 1971 of the murder of "at least 22" Vietnamese noncombatants, a Harris Poll revealed that an incredible 91 percent of its respondents had followed the trial closely. Among those polled, 36 percent disagreed with the verdict, 35 percent agreed, and 29 percent were undecided.

A Horrendous Tragedy

The crime in which Calley participated was one of the most horrendous atrocities in the history of U.S. warfare. The initial charges against Calley accused him of personally killing or ordering to be killed 109 civilians on March 16, 1968, but the total killed that day far exceeded that gruesome number. One of the men later described the scene:

> I just killed. I wasn't the only one that did it; a lot of people in the company did it, hung 'em, all types of ways, any type of way you could kill someone that's what they did. That day in My Lai I was personally responsible for killing about twenty-five people. Personally, I don't think beforehand anyone thought that we would kill so many people. I mean we're talking about four to five hundred people. We almost wiped out the whole village, a whole community. I can't forget the magnitude of the number of people that we killed and how they were killed, killed in lots of ways.

> Do you realize what it was like killing five hundred people in a matter of four or five hours? It's just like the gas chambers—what Hitler did. You line up fifty people, women, old men, children, and just mow 'em down. And that's the way it was—from twenty-five to fifty to one hundred. Just killed. We just rounded 'em up, me and a couple of guys, just put the M-16 on automatic, and just mowed 'em down.

Although the words *My Lai* and *massacre* will forever be

linked in the historical record, the enormity of the evil of that day is scarcely remembered. For many Americans, it is one of a host of unpleasant and uncomfortable images and associations from the Vietnam War that they seek to forget. As the divided public reaction to the Calley verdict also revealed, the explanation of what happened was elusive and has continued to confound those who seek to understand and to ease the psychic pain of the evil and horror of Vietnam. Who was responsible and who was to blame? Time has a way of healing, according to the old adage. Time also erases or blurs memories. Forgetting and healing are not necessarily synonymous.

Accepted Facts

Some facts about My Lai are generally accepted. On March 16, 1968, troops of Charlie Company, First Battalion, Twentieth Infantry Brigade, Americal Division combat air assaulted a village in South Vietnam's Quang Ngai Province. Known to Americans as My Lai 4, Vietnamese called it Thuan Yen. It was part of a hamlet called Tu Cung, which was part of a larger village called Son My. In GI slang it was "Pinkville," a name derived from shading on military maps that indicated a densely populated area.

Charlie Company was part of Task Force (TF) Barker, a temporarily assembled strike unit of three infantry companies and an artillery battery commanded by Lieutenant Colonel Frank Barker. TF Barker's mission was to locate and destroy Vietcong main-force combat units in an area that had long been a political and military stronghold for the enemy. Captain Ernest L. Medina commanded Charlie Company and Second Lieutenant William L. "Rusty" Calley commanded the company's First Platoon.

Shortly before 8:00 A.M., helicopters landed the company outside My Lai. Expecting Vietcong resistance, the first and second platoons entered the village with weapons firing. By noon every living thing in My Lai that the troops could find—men, women, children, and livestock—was dead. The total of Vietnamese civilians killed numbered 504, according to North and South Vietnamese sources. The casualties of Charlie Company were one self-inflicted gunshot wound in the foot. The company's report to the division commander, Major General Samuel W. Koster, listed 128 enemy killed in action (KIA) and three weapons captured. Two days later, the division's newsletter proclaimed: "TF Barker Crushes Enemy Stronghold.". . .

Three Explanations

In examining the My Lai massacre, three explanations emerge. Although they tend to point the finger of blame in three directions, they are complementary and, in combination, help reveal who or what was responsible. One explanation is that a mental breakdown by some individual members of Charlie Company produced this atrocity. The culprit is emotion, ranging from fear, rage, and vengeance on one extreme to no human feeling at all on the other. This interpretation cites mounting psychological pressures on the men. On February 12 a bullet from an unseen sniper had killed Specialist Four Bill Weber. His death was the company's first in Vietnam. Over the next month there were more deaths and terrible wounds from land mines and booby traps, but no face-to-face encounters with enemy troops. The men became increasingly brutal in their treatment of Vietnamese civilians they encountered on their patrols, and the officers tolerated this behavior. On March 15 the company held an emotional memorial service for Sergeant George Cox, a popular squad leader who had been blown apart by a booby trap the previous day. Immediately after the service, Medina briefed the men on the next morning's operation at My Lai. The service and briefing merged into a kind of ritualistic preparation for bloody vengeance. Regardless of what were Medina's specific orders before going into My Lai, the troops were primed to kill, and kill they did. For some the villagers were the unseen enemy that had been killing and maiming their friends for weeks, and for others the victims were scarcely human at all. The soldiers' behavior was so shocking that attention can be misdirected toward them and shifted away from what others were doing.

Poor leadership is a second explanation for the atrocity, and it puts the burden primarily on the company, battalion, and division officers. Medina, Barker, Colonel Oran K. Henderson (the new brigade commander supervising his first combat operation), and Koster are the chief culprits here. Calley himself fits both the first and second explanation, because his rank gave him command responsibility while his inexperience made him susceptible to breakdown. Either from actual orders or from the informal climate in the division, many of the men believed they had license to kill. Ridenhour suspects that the higher officers may purposefully have planned an operation to brutalize the village and others. A similar, somewhat smaller, and never fully prosecuted incident occurred with Bravo Company of TF Barker at the nearby village of My Khe. In this counterterrorism scenario, a brutal attack on a village in a Vietcong-controlled area would be a demonstration to the local people, something like a criminal gang burning out a small business to convince others in the neighborhood to pay protection money. It is likely that Henderson and Koster were in "Charlie-Charlie" (command and control) helicopters over My Lai, and it is certain that Medina and Barker were close by. Did these officers make no move to stop the ground action because it was going according to plan? Even if not planned, Colonel William Eckhardt, who supervised the My Lai prosecutions, notes that Medina quickly knew the men were on a rampage and did nothing to stop it. Medina and those above him may have kept a discreet distance to create plausible deniability later.

A third explanation is that the massacre flowed from what could be called the American way of war in Vietnam. The United States used high technology and vast material resources to inflict maximum suffering and damage on the enemy while minimizing pain and loss to U.S. forces. Military historian Russell Weigley has noted that "war creates a momentum of its own; the use of violence cannot be so nicely controlled and restrained as strategist . . . would have it." The culprit is body count or kill ratio—that is, counting the number of enemy KIA or comparing enemy KIA to American KIA. In a war where the enemy often wore civilian clothes, the bodies were often counted using the "mere gook rule" that "if it's dead and it's Vietnamese, it's VC." Secretary of Defense Robert McNamara's Pentagon devised this war by the numbers, and General William C. Westmoreland, the commander of all forces in Vietnam, tried to implement it through an attrition strategy sometimes labeled "search and destroy." The destruction was accomplished not just by soldiers' firing into villages with M-16s and rocket-propelled grenades (RPGs), but also by artillery, napalm bombs, and B-52 carpet bombing in so-called "free-fire zones." All of this violence was the product of a global strategy to deter the ambitions of America's powerful enemies. How many Vietnamese civilians had to die to prove a point to Moscow and Beijing? What point was being proved? There was no relationship between means and ends. . . .

The Aftermath

These three considerations are important in trying to obtain some closure as to how this atrocity could have happened, but of equal or even greater long-term significance is the aftermath, including the cover-up, uncovering, trials, and finally the response of the military and the public. The dark secret of March 16 was held within the Americal Division for a year. A complaint by Warrant Officer Hugh C. Thompson, Jr., had been forwarded up the brigade chain of command almost immediately. A helicopter pilot, Thompson was not part of Charlie Company but was in the aviation unit assigned to cover the ground assault on My Lai. Realizing what the ground forces were doing, he landed and rescued the few civilians he could. The actions of Thompson and his crew were a singular and powerful expression of compassion and moral courage amid a scene of human depravity. His formal report of brutal and unprovoked murder of civilians was not investigated or acted upon by brigade or division headquarters. Did the senior officers in charge simply not believe the brash young pilot? Had they become insensitive to violence against civilians? Were they knowingly hiding their own culpability and failure of leadership?

The uncovering began more than a year after the event, when Ron Ridenhour, a recently discharged GI, wrote a letter. He sent copies to the army and to several members of Congress. It asked for a public investigation of "something very black indeed," namely, the possible killing of every man, woman, and child in the village of My Lai. Without this letter, the crimes at My Lai might never have been investigated. Ridenhour had not been in Charlie Company or at My Lai, but he knew several men who were. He had heard them describe that day in chilling detail. His sense of justice and patriotism compelled him to track down other witnesses, to search for more grim facts, and ultimately to speak out. In his letter he quoted Winston Churchill: "A country without a conscience is a country without a soul, and a country without a soul is a country that cannot survive."

Numerous investigations ensued. The Department of the Army Inspector General and the Criminal Investigation Division of the Army determined, largely through interviews with members of Charlie Company and other witnesses such as Thompson and his crew, that the laws of land warfare had been violated. General Westmoreland, who was then Army Chief of Staff, created a special investigation panel headed by Lieutenant General William R. Peers. With the army's image already damaged by the long and increasingly controversial war in Vietnam, Westmoreland was as concerned about the apparent cover-up by senior officers as he was about rite brutality in the village. Peers returned a stunning report that graphically described the carnage and called for the indictment of twenty-eight officers. At the top of Peers's hit list was General Koster, who had moved on to become commandant of West Point, one of the army's most honored assignments.

Naming suspects and getting convictions proved to be very different propositions. Because many months had passed since the crimes, many of those involved were out of the service, and the Nixon administration's Justice Department resisted bringing civilians before military courts-martial. Evidence had been destroyed, and key witnesses either could not or would not remember important details. In addition, military law allowed commanders to review the merits of charges brought against members of their command. As a result of these factors, Koster and several other senior officers escaped the court-martial process entirely. Lieutenant General Jonathan Seaman harshly censured Koster for failing to investigate Thompson's complaint and for ignoring other evidence of wrongdoing. In a nonjudicial action, the former Americal commander was demoted to brigadier general and stripped of his Distinguished Service Medal; he soon retired, his once promising career finished. Although Seaman may have been correct that there was not enough evidence to proceed to open trial, the public-relations impact of his decision was enormous. Since Koster's censure was administered privately, the dropping of the formal charges made it appear that one general was simply protecting another and letting others take the blame and punishment for My Lai.

The Story Breaks

From the time that Ridenhour wrote his letter, he had feared the military would not pursue the cases. He began trying to get his story to the press but could find no real interest. After the arrest of Calley in September 1969, an investigative reporter in Washington, Seymour Hersh, began to look into the Calley case, not knowing about Ridenhour or the broader investigation. Slowly the story began to come out. Hersh began publishing a series of reports, and he found Ridenhour, who was a fountain of information. On November 20 the *Cleveland Plain Dealer* published photographs of the massacre taken by Ron Haeberle, a combat photographer who had been present. Shortly afterward, Paul Meadlo appeared on the *CBS Evening News*. The press and public had to acknowledge that something horrible had happened at My Lai.

The story became front-page news, but the initial reaction was disquieting. Many Americans simply refused to believe that the allegations could be true, and others accused the accusers of trying to tear down the armed forces. Thirteen members of Charlie Company, including Captain Medina, were eventually charged with murder. All were acquitted or had their charges dropped except for Calley. Colonel Barker had died in Vietnam in a June 1968 helicopter crash. Twelve officers were accused in the cover-up, but only Colonel Henderson stood trial. He was acquitted after several witnesses declared under oath that they could not recall the events about which they were being questioned.

Calley, then, was the only person convicted of My Lai related crimes. A military court of six officers found him guilty of premeditated murder and sentenced him to life imprisonment at hard labor. Responding to public criticism of the verdict and especially the complaint that this one junior officer was being singled out, Nixon as commander-in-chief moved Calley from the stockade at Fort Benning to house arrest and said he would review the case. Privately, Secretary of the Army Stanley Resor and, publicly, Captain Aubrey Daniel, who had prosecuted Calley, took strong issue with the president's action. They argued that the president's interference denigrated the military justice system and that it placed the U.S. government in the position of condoning a crime that, in Resor's words, stood "alone in infamy." After various appeals and reviews, Calley served only four and a half months in the military prison at Fort Leavenworth.

A Host of Mistakes

Like Resor and Daniel, many military professionals understood that there was no defense or excuse for the cold-blooded mass murder at My Lai. The U.S. military role in Vietnam ended in 1973, and career officers throughout the Army began to take a hard look at the institution to which they remained loyal. Many of them saw a host of mistakes made in management and organization of the military, and they set out to reform the system and restore its fallen honor. In military staff and command schools and colleges, My Lai and the law of war became important subjects of study.

Answers to disturbing questions about My Lai remained difficult to fashion because the event itself was so painful to recall. For many years Americans sought to repress the entire Vietnam War experience in both their own minds and the nation's collective memory. Vietnam, after all, represented defeat and failure. Immediately after the fall of Saigon to North Vietnamese forces in April 1975, President Gerald Ford and Secretary of State Henry Kissinger urged the public to put Vietnam behind them and not to dwell on it or think about it. Many Vietnam veterans, tormented by nightmarish recollections of the fear, rage, and horror that they had been through, wished to God that they could forget.

CHRONOLOGY

January 14: An explosion aboard the aircraft carrier USS *Enterprise* near Hawaii kills twenty-five people.

January 20: Richard Nixon succeeds Lyndon Johnson as president of the United States.

January 30: The Beatles give their last public performance on the roof of Apple records in London. The impromptu concert is interrupted by police.

February 15: Four aquanauts descend fifty feet to a sea lab on the bottom of Great Lameshur Bay in the Virgin Islands to live there for sixty days.

March 3: In a Los Angeles, California, court, Sirhan Sirhan admits that he killed presidential candidate Robert F. Kennedy in 1968. NASA launches *Apollo 9* to test the lunar module.

March 10: In Memphis, Tennessee, James Earl Ray pleads guilty to assassinating Martin Luther King Jr. Ray would later retract his guilty plea.

March 17: Golda Meir of Milwaukee, Wisconsin, becomes the prime minister of Israel.

March 18: The United States begins a secret bombing of Cambodia: 3,650 B-52s drop four times the tonnage of bombs dropped on Japan in all of World War II.

March 24: Lennox Raphael's play *Che* is busted for obscenity.

March 30: A federal jury indicts the Chicago Eight.

April 4: Denton Cooley implants the first temporary artificial heart. The Smothers Brothers television show is deemed "controversial" and canceled.

April 20: Students and volunteers begin building People's Park on an abandoned lot that belonged to the University of California, Berkeley.

May 14: Supreme Court justice Abe Fortas resigns under fire for improper personal conduct.

May 15: The University of California, Berkeley, reclaims People's Park in the face of student and volunteer protest. The police respond with gunfire, killing one student and injuring 128 other protesters.

May 18: NASA launches *Apollo 10.*

June 8: Nixon announces the withdrawal of twenty-five thousand troops from Vietnam by August 31.

June 27: The Stonewall Riot marks the start of the modern gay rights movement.

July 18: Edward M. Kennedy drives off a bridge on his way home from a party on Chappaquiddick Island, Massachusetts. Mary Jo Kopechne, an aide who was in the car with him, dies in the accident.

July 20: *Apollo 11* lands on the moon.

July 25: Nixon declares the Nixon Doctrine, stating that the United States now expects its Asian allies to take care of their own military defense. This was the start of the "Vietnamization" of the Vietnam War.

August 9–10: Sharon Tate and the LaBiancas are murdered. The slayings would be traced to cult followers of Charles Manson.

August 17: Category 5 hurricane Camille hits the Mississippi coast, killing 248 people and causing $1.5 billion in damages.

September 3: North Vietnamese leader Ho Chi Minh dies.

September 24: The trial of the Chicago Eight begins.

October: A rumor spreads that Beatle Paul McCartney is dead.

October 15: Thousands participate in the Vietnam Moratorium.

October 21: Novelist Jack Kerouac dies.

October 30: The U.S. Supreme Court orders immediate desegregation throughout the United States.

November 4: The Chicago Eight become the Chicago Seven as

Black Panther Bobby Seale is removed from the trial for contempt of court.

November 10: The television show *Sesame Street* premieres.

November 15: Thousands march in the Mobilization on Washington.

November 30: U.S. Army lieutenant William Calley is charged with covering up the massacre of 567 civilians by his troops at My Lai, Vietnam, in March 1968. Six hundred Native Americans occupy Alcatraz.

December 1: The first draft lottery is initiated.

December 24: The Manson family murderers are indicted.

FOR FURTHER RESEARCH

Antiwar Movements

Loren Baritz, *Backfire: A History of How American Culture Led Us into the Vietnam War and Made Us Fight the Way We Did.* New York: Morrow, 1985.

Mark Barringer, "The Antiwar Movement in the United States," *Modern American Poetry*, 1998. www.english.uiuc.edu.

Stephanie Brenowitz, "The Conscience of America," *Matrix*, October 2000.

Alexander Cockburn, "To Make Mistakes Is Glorious," *Nation*, April 24, 2000.

Charles DeBenedetti, *An American Ordeal: The Antiwar Movement of the Vietnam Era.* Syracuse, NY: Syracuse University Press, 1990.

Samuel G. Freedman, "They Refused to Fight, Even in the 'Good War,'" *New York Times*, January 13, 2002.

Adam Garfinkle, *Telltale Hearts: The Origins and Impact of the Vietnam Antiwar Movement.* New York: St. Martin's, 1995.

Paul Joseph, "The Antiwar Movement Then and Now," *Peacework*, May 2003. www.afsc.org.

Edward P. Morgan, "From Virtual Community to Virtual History: Mass Media and the American Antiwar Movement of the 1960s," *Radical History Review*, Fall 2000.

Thomas Powers, *The War at Home: Vietnam and the American People.* New York: Grossman, 1973.

Nancy Zaroulis and Gerald Sullivan, *Who Spoke Up? American Protest Against the War in Vietnam, 1963–1975.* Garden City, NY: Doubleday, 1984.

Culture and Counterculture

Vincent Bugliosi, *Helter Skelter: The True Story of the Manson Murders.* New York: W.W. Norton, 1994.

Anne-Marie Cusac, "The Promise of Stonewall," *Progressive*, August 1999.

Mikal Gilmore, "The Sixties," *Rolling Stone*, August 23, 1990.

Arnie Kantrowitz, "What Became the Spirit of '69," *Harvard Gay and Lesbian Review*, Summer 1999.

Kenneth R. Kappel, *Chappaquiddick Revealed: What Really Happened.* New York: SPI, 1989.

Martin A. Lee and Bruce Shlain, *Acid Dreams: The CIA, LSD, and the Sixties Rebellion.* New York: Grove, 1985.

Joel Makower, *Woodstock: The Oral History.* Garden City, NY: Doubleday, 1989.

Don Mitchell, "The End of Public Space? People's Park, Definitions of the Public, and Democracy," *Annals of the Association of American Geographers*, March 1995.

Andru J. Reeve, *Turn Me On, Dead Man: The Complete Story of the Paul McCartney Death Hoax.* Ann Arbor, MI: Popular Culture Ink, 1994.

Richard Sorrell and Carl Francese, *From Tupelo to Woodstock: Youth, Race, and Rock and Roll in America, 1954–1969.* Dubuque, IA: Kendall/Hunt, 1993.

Lionel Wright, "The Stonewall Riots—1969," July 1999. www.socialistalternative.org.

Space Exploration

Buzz Aldrin and Robert Charles, "Apollo 11: The Gift of America's Spirit," *Washington Times*, July 22, 2002.

Douglas Brinkley, "July 20, 1969: 'One Giant Leap for Mankind,'" *Time*, March 31, 2003.

David Darling, *The Complete Book of Space Flight: From Apollo 1 to Zero Gravity.* Indianapolis: John Wiley, 2002.

Leonard David, "The Challenge That Was Apollo," *Aviation Week & Space Technology*, July 18, 1994.

Timothy R. Gaffney, "The Moon Walkers," *Boys' Life*, July 1994.

Howard Lindaman, *Space: A New Direction for Mankind*. New York: Harper & Row, 1969.

Howard Means, "The Eagle Has Landed," *Washingtonian*, July 1999.

Andrew Phillips, "Faded Dreams: Remembering the Moon Landing," *Maclean's*, July 25, 1994.

Frank Sietzen Jr., "America and the Moon: Then and Now," *Ad Astra*, July/August 1999.

The Vietnam War

John Attarian, "Rethinking the Vietnam War," *World & I*, July 2000.

Michal R. Belknap, *The Vietnam War on Trial: The My Lai Massacre and the Court-Martial of Lieutenant Calley*. Lawrence: University Press of Kansas, 2002.

Barbara Crossette, "Vietnam: Second Thoughts," *New York Times*, September 2, 1999.

William J. Duiker, *Ho Chi Minh: A Life*. New York: Hyperion, 2001.

Adam Garfinkle, "The Vietnam War and American Society: Aftermyths of the Antiwar Movement," *Current*, March/April 1996.

George C. Herring, "America and Vietnam: The Unending War," *Foreign Affairs*, Winter 1991.

Jeffrey Kimball, *Nixon's Vietnam War*. Lawrence: University Press of Kansas, 2002.

Michael Lind, *Vietnam: The Necessary War: A Reinterpretation of America's Most Disastrous Military Conflict*. New York: Free Press, 2002.

Robert S. McNamara, *Argument Without End: In Search of Answers to the Vietnam Tragedy*. Boulder, CO: Public Affairs, 1999.

Robert H. Miller, "Vietnam: Folly, Quagmire, or Inevitability?" *Studies in Conflict and Terrorism*, April–June, 1992.

Websites

Billy Shears: The Secret History of the Beatles, www.paul-is-dead. com. This website contains a large amount of information about the popular rock group, including a detailed analysis of the "Paul is dead" rumor.

1969 Woodstock Festival and Concert, www.woodstock69.com. Offering stories, music, and photos, this site gives a comprehensive picture of the monumental Woodstock concert in 1969.

Vets with a Mission, www.vwam.com. This site offers information on the Vietnam War, the ethnic peoples of Vietnam, Vietnam War photos, and much more.

Vietnam War Internet Project, www.vwip.org. This is an educational organization dedicated to providing information and documents about the Vietnam War. It also supports the collection and electronic publication of oral histories and memoirs of those who served and those who opposed the conflict.

INDEX